BARBARA ANN KIPFER

Bestselling Author of *14,000 Things to Be Happy About*

....

4,10

Ways

Nature

Makes Us

Smile

A Guide to Finding Happiness in the Outdoors

FALCON

ESSEX, CONNECTICUT

An imprint of The Globe Pequot Publishing Group, Inc.
64 South Main Street
Essex, CT 06426
www.globepequot.com

Falcon and FalconGuides are registered trademarks and Make Adventure Your Story is a trademark of The Globe Pequot Publishing Group, Inc.

Distributed by NATIONAL BOOK NETWORK

British Library Cataloguing in Publication Information available

Library of Congress Cataloging-in-Publication Data

Names: Kipfer, Barbara Ann, author.
Title: 4,101 ways nature makes us smile : a guide to finding
   happiness in the outdoors / Barbara Ann Kipfer.
Description: Essex, Connecticut : Falcon, [2025]
Identifiers: LCCN 2024041512 (print) | LCCN 2024041513 (ebook) | ISBN
   9781493084265 (paperback) | ISBN 9781493084272 (ebook)
Subjects: LCSH: Nature—Psychological aspects. | Environmental psychology.
Classification: LCC BF353.5.N37 K57 2025 (print) | LCC BF353.5.N37
   (ebook) | DDC 155.9/1—dc23/eng/20250111
LC record available at https://lccn.loc.gov/2024041512
LC ebook record available at https://lccn.loc.gov/2024041513

To Paul, who has hiked, biked, and picnicked with me for decades. I always loved being outside, but it is way more fun with you.

CONTENTS

INTRODUCTION

4,101 Ways Nature Makes Us Smile: A Guide to Finding Happiness in the Outdoors is a mix of entries with the intent of making you feel like you are "right there" experiencing all that nature has to offer. You will feel the force of nature, encounter earth's teachings, and be inspired to find ways to bring more nature into your life. Like a curious child studying things underfoot and within reach, this book's entries are focused on patterns in nature that too often elude us hurried humans. *4,101 Ways Nature Makes Us Smile* is a simulator of nature in book form.

Although modern life has made it easy to lose touch, it is not that hard to reconnect with the rhythms of nature. Though some entries in this book will conjure experiences for you, many others will be unfamiliar yet inspire you to get outside as much as you can. And the premise of this book is supported by best-selling author Richard Louv (*Last Child in the Woods* and *The Nature Principle*), who talks about nature-deficit disorder and the need for Vitamin N (nature). Nature provides significant sources of pleasure for modern humans. You only have to open your eyes to see it, to enjoy it, and to feel it—the incredible riches all around you, every day—and in every page of *4,101 Ways Nature Makes Us Smile*.

This book is meant to inspire readers to keep their own journals or notes in this book about the natural world around them. *4,101 Ways Nature Makes Us Smile* is all about appreciation and respect, a step toward a greener mindset and the first steps in furthering conservation and preservation. Contemplating and learning from nature is what this book is all about.

—Barbara Ann Kipfer

4,101 WAYS NATURE MAKES US SMILE

rock-strewn Arctic desert

the Everglades

a clam at high tide

snow sifting into the trees

oyster shells, thick and castellated

the sun swimming back to the east

Haystack Rock on the Oregon coast

a giant lobelia plant

the first snow sputtering to an end

moonbows (lunar rainbows)

a close-up of the inside of a flower

peppers with their contorted shapes

dawn arriving beyond the trees

squirrels tightrope walking

dried geranium, lavender, and tansy

a huge golden moon

cotton candy-colored flamingos

a lone, lightning-struck tree

zooplankton, usually microscopic

grass, soft underfoot

the shade of a sprawling scrub oak

a bluff of trees on the prairie

fragrant, bee-buzzed flowers

a blue-and-pink sunrise

Dall sheep of the Arctic

the beaver's ability to build

pelicans preening on a dune

a lazy breeze coming off the water

the flower of the willow tree

the various kingdoms of nature

mountains with cloudy eyebrows

the humming of small insects

the perfect harmony of birds in song

rabbits' noses wiggling

lemon and butter-colored roses

rain stopping and sunlight appearing

the bugling of migrating elk

a soothing visit to the sea

the moon lighting the way

venerable maple trees

birds sleeping with one eye open

autumn's natural beauty

breakers pounding the coast

bamboo bending with the wind

a tranquil rainfall

soft sunlight and the colors of fall

a grass spider's web with raindrops

the fur of gray squirrels

the red of cherries

undulating vineyards

black-eyed Susans baking in the sun

rare Florida panthers

a waterfall cascading

the first peach you ever tasted

granite peaks and beechwood forests

wildlife action picking up at night

the tiny green leaves on a strawberry

bushy-tailed gray squirrels

the darkness of a lake at night

mountain birds of prey

a lotus floating on a pond

bedsheet clouds (cirrostratus)

a bumblebee drinking from a flower

underground steam escaping

moles improving soil by aerating it

baby turtles leaving their nests

a garden bursting with color

seedboxes of plants

the squirrel's heartbeat

parrots' head-bobbing

the chitchat of forest homes

a vast underground cave system

aardvarks and anteaters

the first petals on the dogwood tree

a flower under the snow

baboon sanctuaries

landscape charged with rare light

trees making a huge, glowing bouquet

prickly horse chestnuts

corn tassels trembling

a rippling brook running over rocks

nature's constant upheaval

elephants paddling in the river

swallows' autumn flight south

the shimmering of snow crystals

a waterfall's thunder

the flow of waterfalls

an annual pass to the national parks

the little sparrow with the pink beak

ocean water's true colorlessness

birdsong during your walk

sunrise behind Spanish moss

the majesty of orcas

gauzy streaks of cloud

spaniel-eared irises

seed pods and crisp oak leaves

supernova remnants

winter waves frozen along the sand

the most beautiful flower

the vastness of a moonless night sky

topaz, colorless in its pure state

an animal burrowing or digging

the summer solstice

a desert made fertile

sharpened peaks piercing the sky

a sun-dappled glade

fresh-cut lawns' perfume

minnows darting between rocks

wildflowers of winter

a large, double-coned volcano

the horizon of the sea

birds' egg speckling

cherry trees blooming in unison

the unique aroma of each plant species

a hard winter finally softening

the first snowbells

tulips closing their shutters at night

the strength of the mountains

cormorants en masse

smooth sea ice that is safe to walk on

a cold rain after hot, humid days

the slow flapping of herons

hot sun on your shoulders

the woods bright when the moon is full

deified forces of nature

trees cellophaned in sleet

a budding weeping willow

deer drinking at water's edge

a parrot's vocabulary

the promise of twilight

rain forest canopy

the primacy of trees

a barnyard full of animals

eerie rock formations

snowdrops and daisies in bloom

an ended heat wave

aboveground plants like peas

hummingbirds flying backwards

the earthy smell after a spring rain

snails carrying their homes

wildebeests migrating

a caterpillar looking for food

a small rose beginning to bloom

butterflies playing tag

the oldest images of plants—fossils

a crozzled old sycamore

the trilling of a bird

crystals growing in a cave

birds building a nest

the woodsy smell of violets

an aerial view of a pumpkin patch

pewter and silver olive trees

clear mountain air

a bloom as white as bone

nature's summer abandon

a whale-watching event

ginkgo trees in a riot of yellow

the rounded geometry of a spider's web

black frost, so cold the fields smoke

animals aimlessly taking their time

an aasvogel circling high above

wild goats running amok

redwoods of cathedral height

a wild bog of cranberries

mornings of berries and fog

the gentle falling of autumn leaves

a dwarf peperomia

soft, shifting sands

the mutter of distant thunder

a yellow Labrador retriever

lobsters' and crabs' ten legs

boarlets in the woods

blooms of lettuce coral

acres of redbud trees

a row of ducklings

the translucence of mica

the colorful Atlantic puffin

a trail sketched by animal paws

the sky seeming vast for a moment

pinon- and juniper-covered foothills

brilliant white polar caps

a river with three feet of ice

tiny mauve lavender flowers

a canyon at sunrise

a thunderstorm in February

bare toes in a cold stream

a frosted, stem-tangled meadow

oak trees throwing mast

three-toed jacamar

the expansiveness of the ocean

daisies in the breeze

an orangey ember cavern

the smooth back of a horse

lightning's gleaming rod

pears hanging invitingly over a wall

ice crystals on holly leaves

lilac sunsets with a sunflower sun

a brook racing along after rain

the cycles of rain and evaporation

the dusky shapes of shrubs

the blue aerodrome of the sky

plovers acting on instinct

Antarctica mountains

the color of the inside of a blueberry

a snail inside its shell

stones sitting alone in the moonlight

volcanic island arc systems

the roots of a rose bush

a most elegant sunset over calm water

the chatter of darting starlings

nature's pandemonium

birds chirping in the morning

a really cold day in June

twigs knobbed with buds

fields of sunflowers

baby chicks scurrying underfoot

newly denuded trees

a bird on the wing

the deep history of our planet

the exuberant rushing of spring rivers

whitecaps on a summer sea

trails of blackberry

thickets bordering the meadow

the rituals of a cat

white clouds suspended in a blue sky

lilac trees unfurled

excited rustling behind the hedges

a sunset-through-the-trees view

ants' work ethic

the wonder of an egg

Audubon's Great Backyard Bird Count

fields full of daffodils

an orchard of fruit trees

trees dancing with the wind

berries, beautiful in the sunlight

wind ebbing and strengthening

old squirrels and young deer

bucolic nature scenes

oak leaves clinging, curled

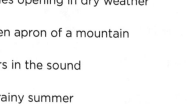

nature becoming colorized

the blue stage of the sky

a periwinkle sunset

pinecones opening in dry weather

the green apron of a mountain

sandbars in the sound

a cool, rainy summer

wild cherry's ringed/banded bark

ocean bashing its cymbals on rocks

woods dark with evergreens

a bird chorus at 4 a.m.

an actively accreting river delta

autumn bird-watching

a nesting crab or plump clam

a flock of flamingos pinking by

the squirting of clams

a bell pepper's inner chambers

remnants of a tumultuous volcanic past

a fracture zone in ice

Charolais cattle grazing beside goats

fluffy white clouds

the colors of nature

cotton-candy clouds

a rollicking flock of blackbirds

birds in refuge, fallen silent

a brilliant day after a storm

the fresh green of turnip leaves

the silhouette of a dandelion

a cardinal in red velvet

leafy sprays of daisies and wild roses

trees prepared for winter

light dappling a trickling stream

the whistles of a single cardinal

small windfall apples

skunks hibernating

the golden glow of a harvest moon

a vivid angelfish

firmly planted roots

a steamy rain forest

birds eating berries off the bushes

cranberries in bud

rain hitting the pavement

a French bulldog's wrinkly face

honeysuckle reaching upwards for light

a scurry of squirrels

contours of surrounding hills

the butterfly's loping flight

light hitting a cobweb at the window

a teeming mass of penguins

the common rosefinch

the scent of rainwater filling the air

a pebble brook chattering with cold

rows of newly potted seedlings

a river bathed in mist

gardens sparkling after rain

a spider's mandala-like web

anemones waving from a coral reef

buds tightly furled

snow-covered stone walls

blue-point Siamese cats

the praying mantis

twilight through thin trees

the fragrance of hot sun

the healing power of nature

bright green foliage

white, night-blooming orchids

a blackbird bobbing for crab apples

sun on mountaintops

a plant's common name

the Latin names of clouds

the thickness of Antarctica's ice

an aerie, the nest of any bird of prey

the 6,000 known minerals (and counting)

fields of ripening grain

a masterpiece of unspoiled nature

any kind of baby animal

seagulls wheeling above in silence

the screaming of ravens

snow thickened on twisted apple trees

petals overlapping petals

the twitter of birds waking

a green-waved lawn

the Allegheny outback

a hornet's nest that is not a threat

buttercups in a golden frenzy

marmots on the trail

horses roaming free

snow swirling out of a black night

Panamint alligator lizards

a fat, luscious pink rose

swans carving still pond waters

great trees attracting the winds

nature in all four seasons

harbor seals pupping on the shores

sea surging into waves

the layers of soil

stripes of snow on the limbs of trees

a twinkling night sky

the groundhog, sitting atop its hole

foliage flitting about in the wind

the meadow or field mouse, a vole

gulls dipping and swooning

an apple tree in winter

hummingbird sightings

the bloom of a prairie pasqueflower

the improvisation of nature

orchards humming happily

a tailgate picnic at a nature center

night sounds answering each other

top fruit from trees

birds enjoying a bath

a horse's distinctive markings

the pink first light of morning

a wave approaching shore

mangroves along tropical coastlines

icefields of the Canadian Rockies

a clear mountain stream

the cherries and strawberries of summer

coastal wilderness

the harbor front's resident pelican

breezes blowing through

the fuzz on rose petals

the earth lightly grilled by the sun

the enchantments of a summer meadow

an urban nature-watch

snow piles before anyone touches them

a slowed chorus of crickets

daisies lifting their faces sunward

bird fights over worms

light, feathery astilbe

kokako, a forest bird of New Zealand

a hen panting with an open mouth

waterfalls spilling down rockfaces

the perfumed tincture of the roses

crabgrass tickling your bare feet

nature's own healing power

a surprise in the garden

earthworms coming to the surface

the nose leather of a cat or dog

Earth's primary climate types

trees bowing over a lake

spruce trees crisp as black paper

the lapping of waves

a dandelion against a bright blue sky

the tail rings on a ring-tailed lemur

the chattering of pebbles

perfectly gray skies

the flight profiles of ducks

camel humps storing fat

daisy heads closing at night

hairless baby mice

a moonlit mottle of sycamores

the migration of birds

deer eating fallen apples

the smell of grapes in a vineyard

tunnels where lava once flowed

the splash of fish in the lake

the pink lip of a seashell

the color of the sky before a storm

a river jumping and splashing

a storm dying down

green twilight in lonely, hushed woods

new buds forming on roses

nature in green variegated dress

rain prints on rocks

a stunning sunrise that lasts a moment

horseback-riding trails

acid-green euphorbia

glorious off-reds of autumn

the smell of strawberries

Japanese cherry trees

the miracle of a dandelion

construction of a termite mound

the moon's mottled face

bachelor's button or cornflower

the aromatic spicebush

star shells on a dark night

bees in their hives

the sound of water on water

the birth of a polar bear

a field of glacial erratics

highbush blueberry plants

limbs of trees encased in ice

Milky Way's outer planets

the smells of the season

perfectly ordered rows of corn

silt forming marshy, shifting islands

pelicans diving for sardines

mangroves' salt-tolerant trees

opportunities to live the outdoor life

the changing angle of the sun

leaves just beginning to expand

variegated Norway maple leaves

stars winking at you

the splash of trout in the shallows

branches about to blossom

a flower unfolding

the sunset as entertainment

sun drenching nature

night wind creaking the eaves

the last rays of sunlight

the observable universe

plum trees in bloom

crisp, white winters

a river's grassy brink

violets' heart-shaped leaves

chipmunks gathering and cracking nuts

a baby duck hatching

breeze classification

warm ocean beaches

nature sculpting our world

the green beans of July

brown wrinkly walnuts

the comma butterfly

stones you can walk across a stream on

a spider hiding out in a barn

100-year-old oak trees

vaquita, a type of short porpoise

dense woodland and snowberries

long, lovely blue days

trees trimmed with dancing leaves

evergreen tree smell

a mountain lion and her cub

the prelude to winter

a lemon-bellied bird

a pebble's smoothness

the solitude of mountainous haunts

flowers taking up water with ease

snowflakes making a very small sound

a swan elegantly floating

the tiny shells of marine mollusks

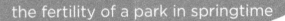
the fertility of a park in springtime

a rolling sea of daffodils

the large holes of the sea clam

the smoothness of sand

the great Andean condor

blackberries, small and shiny black

a bank of wild strawberries

waves' strange push-and-pull

fog misting the violet moors in spring

flower petals overlapping

the northern white rhinoceros

the hoot of a great horned owl

an alligator's long tail

a buffalo's bugle beard

the cold creaking of branches

a piping plover and its chick

bamboo shoots after a rain

the yellows and oranges of the maples

a snowcapped tree

spectacular, long-distance migrations

the smell of gardenia

the rays which paint the landscape

sandy rain skirling along a beach

bulls not actually seeing red

the pebbled beach of a lake

hummingbird visitors

a single pink tulip in bloom

a dreamy crescent of beach

brown, withered ginger root

frogs eating with their eyes closed

bee buzz and hummingbird fizz

a bottomless blue glassy spring

the catfish's 27,000 taste buds

snow on the first day of spring

meerkats sitting up

a waterhole fed by rain and snowmelt

birds doing elegant swooping flybys

frogs splashing and croaking

a cold front coming in

the color of ripe grass

fog softening the sea

the rhythm of waves

the blue-white shadow of a snowy hedge

flamingos, pink from eating shrimp

sunlight warming a plant

open water between ice floes

chestnut burrs plopping to the ground

trees laden with ripened fruit

natural autumn haze

dark cypress trees

the immense bounty of nature

a hovering hummingbird

Sunday afternoon nature walks

life in the hadal zone

the appeal of the forest

the squalls of northern harbors

a wide-open flower

a perverse platypus

sunshine replacing the clouds

clusters of tiny Champagne grapes

cherry trees laden with fruit

a choice of short local nature trails

compost giving birth to flowers

the salutation of the dawn

moonlight casting shadows

serene natural beauty

the power of a thunderstorm

a wild turkey behind your house

cliffs layered with Earth's past

the breeze before a shower

what a hovering eagle sees

a field of swaying seagrass

tropical forest margays

Earth's mysterious hum

cow eyes in a green meadow

oxen sleeping like sphinx

little birds chasing big birds

a horse nuzzling one's palm

musk oxen adapting to the cold

a tent of dropping clouds

the garbled honking of autumn geese

the timelessness of rocks

birds quieting in the heat of day

tiger stripes and leopard spots

plants having best friends

shadows moving over wheat

an island on a moonlit night

vitamin N = nature

river rocks worn smooth

a gray-hooded evening

rock worn or rubbed away by friction

how ladybugs retract their wings

the dark shoulders of the trees

dawn in the mountains or hills

street trees noisy with songbirds

clouds in the sunshine

hickory nuts' heavy shells

a thunderstorm carrying away the heat

the transiency of the clouds

the rich smell of cedar

the damp earth after rain

palms and orange trees

beach rocks with holes

rain bringing out the green

a heron's awesome nest

57 degrees, the happiest temperature

rhapsodic descriptions of nature

songbirds migrating at night

the beauty of fungi

a scattering of starfish

the first day at the beach

a group of peacocks, an ostentation

ancient rocks shaped by the elements

a season that's short but sweet

a 2,000-year-old rain forest

leaves a deep matte green

spruce needles and timothy grass

the opening eyelids of the morn

the sky full of flying leaves

tuff hills and cave dwellings

every molecule pregnant with a mystery

pluot, a plum and apricot hybrid

the brightest sun on whitest snow

the golden gleam of a star

animal tracks that zigzag

a hawk on a slipstream

fox kits emerging from their den

specimens of pond life

rain-soaked birds drying in the sun

deer's infrared vision

beautiful views of the sea

mountains' dark blue silhouette

the silver variety of goldfish

white clover asleep in the meadow

the constellations shifting position

the smell of rivers

ivy twisting around oaks

spiderwebs trembling in the grass

a crimson setting sun

tiny flowers hidden in the grass

a creek lined with daylilies

cloud-gazing as a kind of meditation

a tree extending its roots

giant tortoises going slow and low

Belgian horses grazing patiently

gardenias' strong scent

hundreds of salamanders underground

a macaw in the wild

a stranded iceberg

El Niño and La Niña phenomena

a rumbling creek or brook

tangles of orange lantana blossoms

a turtle pulling its limbs inward

seals treading water

a huge weeping beech tree

cattail seeds flying from a ripe head

the roots of an ancient beech tree

the amazing complexity of a honeycomb

Mediterranean sunsets

loons bassooning on lonely lakes

fish jumping in the pond

the boom and crash of surf

squirrels scampering off

a heat-erasing cold front

ogives or flow ridges

rock columns in a canyon

an unexpected high-mountain lake

the softness of peony petals

the peeling bark of a tree

light breezes and sweet air

an unforgettable sunset

red-winged blackbirds' cock-a-r-e-e-e

a sea-carved coast

beautiful hillside views

the hoarse bellow of a lake

finback and minke whales

a seed germinating naturally

sun turning grass to gold

rain forests preserved

snow lions dancing

hanami, the Japanese custom of flower-viewing

animals poking around with their noses

the eyes of a cat opening onto a soul

a nest filled with eggs

beach explorations at low tide

the Appalachian Trail end and start

Ceres, a dwarf planet

fat tomatoes on the vine

the sound of fish swimming

green beans ready to be picked

the uptake of water by trees

a cat enjoying chilly fall air

wrinkled salt roses

an ant's staccato scurrying

birdsong in winter

the scent of *Sporobolus*, a grass

a wolf saluting the moon

mangrove driftwood

a strong wind whooshing lilac fume

sunset in the wilderness

pumpkin seeds sown

a leaf starting to turn color

eiderdown-soft snow

the tip of a sunbeam

the formation of dunes

Earth's wobbling axis

frogs on lily pads

orange groves and sea mist

insects seeing the colors of flowers

snow falling on water

the taste of the wind

the breath sounds of small whales

a blue whale in the Arctic

the world's largest deserts

paw prints in the snow

pomegranate trees

a field of wild lupine

mesquite in full bloom

animals playfully wrestling

sap uprushing in a tree

basaltic lava pouring into the ocean

a burst of dahlias

seaweed clinging to rock

gangly moose and curious reindeer

a frozen waterfall

the smell of autumn

a busy woodpecker

mountain butterflies

sound bouncing off high canyon walls

the winter sun's low arc

evening-scented wildflowers

delicate blue-flower flax

birds bursting out of bushes

the soft feathers of a bird's chest

a six-foot-long aardvark

the glasswing butterfly

a yellow kalanchoe

corals and jellyfish

two doves in stylish gray

a waterspout at sea

when the birds begin nesting

rising currents of air

the inner passes of the woods

dandelions polka-dotting the lawn

a pond nestled under a plum tree

the first rabbits of the season

a peregrine falcon in the wild

an appreciation of moss

wildflowers in lush meadows

tulips, butterflies, and ladybugs

baby osprey test flights

rivers driven into serpentine patterns

the muscular drama of the ocean

a tree porcupine sleeping on a branch

the weblike cracks in dried-out mud

a huge chestnut-colored quarter horse

the sky, ready to drop more water

Venus, the brightest celestial object

an otter peeking out of the water

a perfectly rounded stone or pebble

the sea rolling across a pebbly shore

an octopus's three hearts

stripes of sedimentary rock

scents from a traditional herb garden

surf on a sandy shore

forests preserved as forever wild

a cloud-flecked sky

a tree-lined road through fields

a path lain with petals

the beauty of field and farm

the National Park System

prickly blue thistle flowers

a good, clean rain

the wild air's salubrity

the country of the pointed firs

dusk creeping across the lawn

a chorus of frogs and a knot of toads

sugar maple leaves, new and miniature

sheer sandstone walls

a perception of Nature's ubiquity

the peace of wild things

a goblet full of pure morning air

the smallest pig in a litter

foamy waves curling over toes

yellow disks of ox-eyed daisies

the turquoise of the sea

a nor'easter tapering off

beach erased by the tide

the branches of an oak groaning

green expanses leading down to a river

tiger lily freckles

woods frantic with life

a green-clad coast

dogwood blossoms unfurling

sunrise at the South Pole

the intricacies of salt marsh

the separate beauty of each flower

where sand dollars nestle

Linnaeus' Botanical Garden in Sweden

the edge of water on shore

acres of sunflower fields

a stand of tall grasses arched by wind

breeziness on a hot day

the first drops of rain on the roof

tall and thorny raspberry bushes

hollow old yew trees

the mesopelagic zone of the ocean

a brook gurgling on its way to the sea

a delicate pond lily root

Pacific blue marlin, called granders

the clouds thinning out

ancient, gnarled trees

the full Flower Moon

beauty in a night sky

breeze scented by flowers

late February fog from melting snow

nature study retreats

the moon captured among tree branches

tight, shiny dolphin skin

the laying of an egg

the colors of the earth

time-lapse photography of nature

the spire of a redwood

phytoplankton, the pasture of the sea

wind blowing the sands

somewhere where there is snow in June

a sapling in the spring

a chameleon's eyes looking around

an untouched snowfield

bees rummaging in the lavender

the frozen earth yearning for spring

the croak of a raven

the orange of fruit doves

being on the beach at dusk

animals dressed for summer

stones talking to each other

an underground cenote

a red cardinal in an evergreen tree

multicolored strata

octopi turning red when angry

the peaches and sweet corn of August

the air we breathe

a star rising at sunset

stately pines whispering

the veins in leaves

squirrels digging in snow

spiderwebs with dew

the gray indifference of the ocean

saolas, rare forest-dwelling bovine

a shining white moon

a pink-necked green pigeon

maple-leaved viburnum

wildflowers not caring where they grow

the way a leaf holds the light

gardens in full bloom

grass-covered levees in a string bog

turtles sunning on rocks

welcome rain during a drought

the aromas of autumn

the calls of birds from harvest fields

poppies ablaze in the sun

the warmth of sun in winter

birds' chatterbox chorale

dogs sweating through their feet

dunes thick with dune grass

the gray jay of Canada

the flight of the mountain hawk

an island of wildflowers

a peach orchard in your backyard

fish scales flashing under the water

a diamond found in the sand

the smell of apples

the Cat's Eye Nebula

the sky filling with colors

snow buntings during a snowstorm

a Golden Delicious apple with a blush

blue sky after a summer rain

the sky filled with a deep-red sunset

a snow-covered sapling

a business of ferrets

shaggy-footed farm horses

the sporty red fox

a walk through a Christmas tree farm

rain dripping off the leaves

Paepalanthus flowers at sunset

sea cliffs and ivory beaches

the songs of scores of birds

rain and ice tapping at the windows

sand slipping softly under your feet

an unknown beach or unnamed lake

the rushing of great rivers

untouched snowy woodland

the Irish wolfhound

what trees and stones will teach you

striking hydrangea bushes

the ebb and flow of each season

Atlantic puffins' multicolor beaks

the autumn sun setting

first bulbs blooming

aerial views of salt marsh

spruce-studded islands

the riotous colors of tulips

a wolf walking through the snow

starlings' process of roller feeding

a baby gorilla laying on its mother

streams in the desert

blueberry fields and salt marshes

pure yellow or rich orange plumage

the wandering moon

Greenland dwarf willows

burdock, an edible Japanese plant

a bed of long-stemmed tulips

the eyelashes of a giraffe

goose flight formation

irises' fragility and character

woods brown and grayed from rain

the structure of DNA

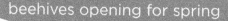

beehives opening for spring

a great heron, perched

the distant presence of the sea

a cloud moving onto a mountain

rose-scented salt air

a rooster within earshot

abalones eating kelp and sea lettuce

giant pink peonies

a dense and uninhabited forest

a reed-lined river

the blessing of birdsong

a conspiracy of lemurs

the footprints of an errant turtle

the first frost of the year

clouds losing their oatmeal heaviness

clean sand and sand dunes

sticky silk lines cast by spiders

great whales in nutrient-rich waters

mushrooms popping up after rain

rain swelling streams and brooks

the softness of dog ears

the swallows' nest in the woodshed

hummingbirds sampling flowers

deeply grooved bark

tree frog conversations

wet grass in the morning

golden mitsumata blooms

an ancient pine and oak forest

plants for making medicines

a sunflower bundle

plants growing in straight rows

a sea otter grooming

sudden late-afternoon thunderstorms

a cluster of ivy berries

calm water beneath a storm

a barn swallows' loft

tiny Key deer grazing

a beautiful call by a robin

the stillness of a garden in winter

a mysterious strand of seaweed

caves and grottoes

coconut trees near white sand

lofty sycamores shawled in Spanish moss

dew hanging off the tip of a leaf

wild long-horned bulls

goats scaling rockfaces

birds soaring on updrafts

the wistful pleasure of an autumn mist

cats and dogs who are friends

a lily pad with lush pink blossom

sunshine through the windows

the unseen tides of the wind

the checkered shadows of trees

margays in a tropical forest

a field dense with poppies

a bright red bird standing out

the sound of loons

when the hurricane suddenly veers away

nature, forever untidy

horses' noses making steam

glacially sculpted mountains

the tangled green of nature

a deserted beach at midnight

peas in their pods

the joys of a bountiful climate

a desert rose in bloom

birds getting really loud for a minute

sable-vested night

summer's blue jay and raccoon

a full moon filling the sky with light

incredible white sunlight

safe nesting in holly bushes

a raccoon and its babies

an orange peel spraying its fragrance

paired fins of fish

an owl hooting before dawn

a sharp ocean breeze

the blue light of afternoon

fluffy clouds and mountaintops

a sunbaked road and wide-open country

the shelter of rocky canyon walls

trees chanting a canticle in the wind

the night breeze over the mountain

a gently swishing field of grain

the wobbly nose of a tapir

cirrus clouds wisped in a cold sky

the woods alive with light

a bright yellow parakeet

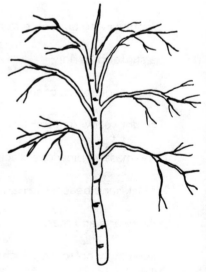

the primeval smell of damp earth

manatees rolling and playing

rich pink parrot tulips

fresh earth, cool snow, pine boughs

unusual and exotic blooms

igneous rock and coves

a spider catching a fly

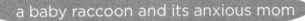
a baby raccoon and its anxious mom

fall foliage day trips

blooms of yuccas and agaves

an ice storm creating glass figurines

the soft fur of a cat

rabbits living under the front porch

a sunset bike ride

the hoarse barks of seals

bright yellow daffodils

the massive plow of a glacier

black sand beaches in Hawaii

liverworts and mosses

seemingly bottomless lochs

backlit maple leaves

a wind blowing across the plains

fossils being formed

bluebirds wrestling with worms

a fresh breeze on a muggy day

a sugar-white sand beach

the hidden life within a field

the smell of carnations

a bright little fish darting about

clouds and mountains commingling

a lavender flower with purple veins

the leaves unfurling on a tree

a blue eye in a cloudy sky

alpacas and humming sheep

the curving, winding neck of a swan

sun lighting a meadow in patches

blue-gray overcast sky

a sea urchin skeleton

a state with thousands of lakes

a breeze off the water

the air cooling as the sun sets

channels on the flank of an iceberg

buds fluttering open

a hummingbird shimmering

the massiveness of mountains

the warmth of the sand on your feet

chipmunks scampering with tails high

a sand dune more than 200 feet high

moonrise over a mountain

bleached winter grass blades

herders' trails along cliffs

rabbits that only play in your garden

the banks of a mountain stream

volcanic pedestals supporting atolls

shadows on the sand

biosphere; literally, "life ball"

remote wilderness landscapes

the color of wet sand

dandelion heads bobbing

indoor blooms brightening winter days

the curves of a shell

the beneficence of nature

geese stirring in the poultry yard

the awe of a simple rainbow

apple buds at the fringe of the wood

a waterfall that falls in stages

the drunken screams of blue jays

swarms of dragonflies

the wind-bruised sea's folds of blue

psychedelic bands of sedimentary rock

clover that has blossomed

wind whistling over stone

rainbow eucalyptus trees

an air chamber under the ice of a pond

basins hollowed for lakes

worms thriving in the dark

the solitude of a falling leaf

the forest: a sweet, dark secret

nature at nighttime

a moon peeking through clouds

a line of green cottonwoods

the windy red geology of Mars

a gecko's mating dance

autumn's gifts stirring the senses

the alpine flowers

all the fish in the sea

snow's pure whiteness

the gnarled quality of bark

a forest covered in newly fallen snow

a hermit crab running away

sunbeams sifting through forest canopy

the whistling call of a blue whale

ribbed sand on the bottom of the sea

fascination with caterpillars

a mass of bushes or brambles

the black silhouettes of trees

a rose in the rain

Jupiter's Great Red Spot

the fragile immediacy of flowers

a cool night breeze

dolphins sleeping with one eye open

sweet corn growing

dusk turning to darkness

lava tubes in volcanic caves

false dawn or zodiacal light

a fresh, cooling lava crust

the sway of a burro

clouds weaving cobwebs across the moon

mists muting leaves' colors

big clumps of clouds

the sun shining during a rain

birds sitting quietly in the heat

yellow lichen growing in a ring

the deep voice of a stream

that ants never sleep

a cow in a corncrib

a sea of grass waving in the wind

where land, sea, and sky meld

a mountain's cone frosted with snow

the fragrances of fruit

any animal running free

a rumbling afternoon thunderstorm

snow swooping down in a hush

a cave lit by glowworms

alpine forget-me-nots

intensely colored wildflowers

cat whiskers, called vibrissae

mountains with autumn colors

the smell of a lush field

trees arched thick over the road

classification of clouds

frost flowers and snow donuts

ferns curling and uncurling

the inspiration of spring

a glint of bare rock

warm sands and turquoise oceans

a shimmer on still waters

frogs jumping and toads walking

the snout of a glacier

that wide-eyed look on a cat

plants in the antlers of stags

the aardvark's long, sticky tongue

cold fall afternoons

lady's slipper uncurling

horseback riding in the snow

geese talking to each other

a family of otters

plants bursting into flower

jungle gardens reminiscent of Amazonia

the various colors of a tree's bark

a hot, glowing fountain on a lava lake

big flowering jasmine plants

the majestic indigo of a lake

Baffin Bay's shores

marsh grasses growing up in a river

the piney, smoky nature of thyme

a hidden clutch of eggs

the colors of oceans

a ragged border of marsh plants

the damp netherworld of spiders

baby goats, wobbly on their Q-tip legs

dark volcanic sand

a sprig of blackberry

a percussion of raindrops

the smell of a forest after rain

places that are unmappable

crevasse fields on a glacier

the purple inside of a clam shell

a cloud of miniature pink fairy roses

the shape of a tree

colors—the smiles of nature

feathers on the beach

sudden, quick thunderstorms

the continental shelf

the record of the rocks

open views of the sea

purple anemone heavy with honeybees

elderberries hanging in heavy clusters

beaded streams on the tundra

the sweet smell of western azaleas

marigolds like shaggy suns

fossils in the Grand Canyon

the silence of the first snow

the way sunlight comes and goes

a moose trotting down the street

the stages of a dandelion's life cycle

animal tracks left in mud

a reflection of a bird in flight

the anatomy of storms

a lizard on a sun-washed rock

a marine mammal paradise

the lilies of the field

moonlight on the ocean

an acorn waiting to be an oak

a path tilting gently downhill

the iron roots of mountains

five-story sea cliffs

a mighty narwhal tusk

dawn's silver frost on the lawn

the purplish-black of elder

the way light loves quartz

the powerful movements of a horse

a panda in the wild

the timid light of spring

sea lions, loud and gregarious

wind roaring across a steppe

polka-dot *Hypoestes*

boulders studding a coastline

the temperature inside a cucumber

banks of marjoram in flower

a dense hummock of forest

a garden like Monet's

lilacs in the park

a petrified tree 20 million years old

when water sparkles at sunset

the bottom of the sea

the bumps of a raspberry

buttercups tossing their heads

trees that invite climbing

the purple petals of an iris

crocus blossoms in early spring

the rusty yellow of ripening corn

spiders spinning webs in corners

nature closing the year in style

the first chill hint of winter

the circle of a crater pit

caves, a time machine of nature

a chick breaking out of its shell

the call of a white-throated sparrow

a spider's tiny brain

wild mustangs in stallion-led herds

the dark blues of a winter sky

neatly striped fields of silage corn

the patterns in running water

a biodiversity hot spot

a field of crocuses

midnight horseback riding

the forest holding its breath

datura growing on the shores

black bears heading to winter dens

the poetry of the earth

Earth Day celebrations

the screams of seagulls

the lighting up of the mist by the sun

stalks of ripe grain bending low

stringybark, Australian eucalypts

flowers lining the walk

an incrispated fern, stiffly curled

a sunny, blue-sky winter's day

the pale dusk of impending night

fragrant white almond blossoms

cheetah cubs climbing trees

volcanic verdigris on the ocean floor

the crest of a linear dune

the daily dramas of light and weather

a dandelion ready to be wished on

clouds in their haloes at dawn

fizzy air before a storm

the panting of a dog

the edge of driftwood along a beach

a daisy laden with dew

the rustle of a tree in a mild breeze

pines against the blue sky

small weeds flowering in January

dense, third-growth fir

the full moon and its aura

blossoms poking through rocks

planets twinkling at night

the distant roar of the wind

salt streaks on a lake

wind-combed fields of goldenrod

ocean touching the sky

a pitch-black night

sulfur needles on a volcanic gas vent

sunset on the lake

animals readying for winter

birch and poplar leaves, soft as gauze

the yellowing green of unripe lemons

the sky the day after a storm

beaches white as lingerie ruffles

a night rimmed with stars

seed and soil flowing into one another

alpine strawberries

glorious gardens with secluded benches

the ability to navigate by the stars

land swept by the sun

an apparently endless forest

rabbit brush, a plant

the craters of the moon

Scandinavian fjords

the blue of the awakening horizon

great shaggy grizzly bears fishing

tulips and warm breezes

crisp ocean spray and cool sea breezes

when a cat hugs you back

slack tide before the turn of the tide

the slender trunks of young trees

when the ice on the ground melts

the volume of water in the oceans

the fur under a cat's chin

pockmarks in the snow

the yellowy color of evening light

strata of mountains, soils, and rocks

seeds of summer under the snow

nature's teeming tapestry

the bloom upon a peach

the wind groaning through the pines

a saturated set of predawn hues

fluffy ruffle ferns

a leaf turning color, here and there

the curvature of the earth's surface

the relentless percussion of the sea

bison cropping the pastures

nuts and berries for animal food

a fluffy little lamb

moss, ferns, and wildflowers

old-growth beech forest

a storm beginning out at sea

a bird-friendly backyard

the lure of a garden path

orange, purple, and white crocuses

bulbs pushing through frigid ground

the seashore on a sunny day

the blue jay in winter plumage

dandelion seeds floating

atmosphere sweet with silence

the abundance of art found in nature

tulips standing at attention

the caw of a lonely bird in flight

ruby-hued blueberry fields

the lemurs of Madagascar

the hot breath of summer wind

a suddenly topaz bay

fog rolling in off the lake

a still-secret island

weeds that look like flowers

where narwhals cavort and whales spout

the barred owl's haunting cry

the end grain of wood

gophers popping up out of holes

a walk on the dunes

trees budding and blooming

pomegranates' jewel-like seeds

a coniferous forest

seeds getting proper stratification

a farmer with a fertile field

the woods quietly renewing themselves

a hound dog dozing in the heat

miniscule pygmy marmosets

coyote faces lifted to the sky

silvery schools of minnows

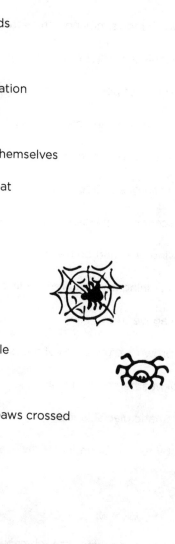

a strutting peacock

palm trees growing at an angle

autumn leaves backlit by sun

sheepdogs slumbering with paws crossed

antelope jackrabbits

rumbles from glacier shifts

stars on a clear night

hot springs bubbling

groundhogs among the lilies

stridulation, the noise of crickets

the colors of an oriole

cloud shadows moving across the land

an exquisite pocket of primeval nature

the sound of pebbles washed by surf

the swishing sound made by oats

a wet seed wild in the hot, blind earth

subtle surges of tide

the scent of night-blooming jasmine

no wind or sound on the moon

surf crashing on pink granite cliffs

blue agave trees

the brown, earthy tones of moose hide

long-weathered tree trunks

a dramatic glacial lagoon

a baby red fox bounding away

fireballs, meteors, asteroids

green grass peeking through snow

a green mound of moss

pumpkin seeds sprouting

a grape arbor with beehives under it

details of a rock in bright sunshine

an undeveloped flower or leaf

sunlight attenuated by clouds

garrigue and maquis scrubland

a polar vortex in May, June, or July

ancient slope-shouldered willow trees

pale frosted roses

the primeval rhythms of the seashore

soft, powdery sand

sheep to trim the grass

the sunny side of the mountain

a whiff of a garden

a crescent moon kissing the horizon

waves crashing around your legs

millions of galaxies

nests that hang, like sporrans

spots of sunlight on the walkway

leaves blowing across snow

peppermint sea stars

the serpent's subtle slither

riotous rainbows of tropical fish

the magic of the Northern Lights

sheep in clumps, like cloud banks

icicles and snow-blanketed ledges

the sun seeping over the horizon

a honey badger in the wild

nature never making haste

fungi on a birch tree

a butterfly running into you

cats hearing ultrasound

the singing of unseen birds

a white path of pebbles

the frigatebird in a powered dive

a breeze fingering your face

blue, blue skies on white, white days

a lion springing in the jungle

a smooth brown rabbit

the swirling layers of a gneiss pebble

a wildflower paradise

open country and uncultivated fields

the V-flight of migrating geese

a bird's nest in your tree

a mirror-smooth lake in early morning

Half Dome in Yosemite

long rollers wrinkling a dark bay

puddles and moss in the dirt

glazed-eyed night owls

storms crackling along mountain ridges

the sound of rain hitting leaves

the fresh scent after it rains

young crickets tuning up

glaciers of the mountain ranges

all the shades of a forest

gray mountains draped with snow

abalone and mother-of-pearl

bright green duckweed

the music of a lagoon

the sun setting in colored ribbons

gnarled tree roots

the uninhibited sounds of wild animals

bunches of daffodils

potato fields and pumpkin patches

Pacific rollers breaking on the beach

horsetails, club mosses, and ferns

the seeds of coco de mer

a cool mist rolling in over the waters

steam from horses' noses

a tiny tributary of a stream

night cool drawing in

animal young names

happy marsupials, like the quokka

hatchlings, little balls of fluff

rabbits wide-eyed in their burrows

bitter northern cold

brown-headed cowbirds

magnificent stands of birch

the tooting of gulls

sika deer (miniature elk)

animals blending into the scenery

a lagoon-smooth leeward beach

the eerie murmur of pigeons

an 80-degree day with no humidity but a breeze

when a butterfly lands on you

landscape gardening

dragonflies stitching organdy air

playful newborn lambs

fossils of previously unknown species

weather-beaten mums

fresh violets in the woods

the green leaves of the hawthorn

wildflowers stippling banks of a bog

the squish of soaked grass

shrubland overlying bedrock

the joy of a sun bath

patterned snow on a mountain

water smoothing a rock in a riverbed

salty breezes by the sea

the sloshing of ocean waves

the branches of a tree

dark clouds blowing over

a sanctuary for disappearing fauna

seeds you can't wait to plant

the sky, blue and unclouded

a cat chirping at the birds

the fruit and shade of the date palm

a private beach with hidden coves

molten snow upon naked mountains

the huge waters of the sea

elephantine granite boulders

superbloom season in the desert

a shoreline walking trail

stone walls and wildflowers

foam on the water, dew on grass

fiery dahlias and playful sunflowers

a comet breaking the sound barrier

a passing bird's squawk

anytime when there are no ticks

butterflies' favorite flowers

a natural rock formation

a shrub's rough bark

sun reflected on snow

a soft leaf on a great tree

baby robins squawking for food

clouds' oatmeal heaviness

ornamentals in flower beds

an island brushed by Atlantic waves

the sky as a movie screen

fall flowers blooming on the vine

nature's sounds unimpeded

the pearl hidden in an ugly shell

a cow meditating on the grass

ancient mountains mellowed by time

an unopened blue globe-thistle

desperately needed rain

a robin's welcome call

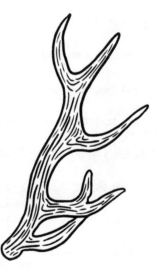

the creak of tall trees on a windy day

the changing seasons

boxwood sparring with the breeze

fluid sap spreading in each tiny leaf

the moist fresh stillness of the woods

birds singing with nature

lavender in the meadow

tree roots crisscrossing the trail

the delightful mood of spring

whale fossils in the desert

an annular eclipse

an enormously beautiful sky

sun setting on colored leaves

a solitary walk in the rain

crisp mountain air

large apricot and orange tulips

deer waiting for their food to defrost

a clear sky on a chilly night

the species not yet discovered

a light sweet breeze

rabbits alert in uncut grass

the rocks in which minerals are buried

the spines of an urchin

dolphins diving playfully

dawn vapors drifting above a pond

the large hood of the merganser

a dense network of glacier streams

a full-blown fall fog hanging in space

earth laughing in flowers

sheep on high-altitude ridges

moonlight on water

the ruckus of birdsong

the placement of seeds in a sunflower

bluebirds eating out of your hand

the last bolt of lightning

holes in trees where birds nest

opossums and bats sleeping upside-down

a bald eagle scouting for fish

core fruits, like the apple and pear

the black-cheeked lovebird

miniature woodland creatures

rain droplets on flower petals

the dry scent of autumn

daylight after the darkness

mountains and wide skies

a turtle scaling rapids

when the woods come alive

rich green fields and dark black soil

the prophecy of clouds

glimpses of dancing lemurs

a morning breeze fingering new leaves

forests coated with transparent ice

a jungle of climbing vegetation

an ocean wave's salty baptism

the commitment of a penguin couple

Neptune, the blue planet

tropical cloud forests

great monolithic rocks of a coast

the smell of wet moss

the mane of the black lion

bird colonies on cliffs

a maze of drifting, misshapen bergs

clouds that seem weightless

the jagged edge of a mirrory lake

the course of a river

pink daisies suddenly springing up

brooks with copper ferns

cow-dotted pastures

a four-leaf clover

copper beech trees standing sentinel

the banana, the largest herb

sunflowers with heads held high

double digging to cultivate soil

blustery Antarctic winds

a purple tint in the horizon

the smell of seaweed

the eyes of a butterfly

idyllic seaside scenes

the graceful curve of a clover's stem

a perfect horseshoe waterfall

the smell of freshly mown meadow hay

cranes crying out in the high clouds

eagles soaring over a canyon

the thousand sounds of the wind

a damask plum or rose

the white underside of a poplar leaf

the long day of planet Mercury

volcanic lightning

the greenness of summer

cave coral or cave popcorn

mountain panoramas

a thousand forests from a single acorn

fresh leaves on a plant

manatees and dugongs

purple slivers of prized amethyst

an owl peering from the treetops

the sound of galloping horses

light dancing off crystals of sand

Earth's primal power

the aromatic softness of old leaves

new clumps of daffodils

pure mountain water

brown bears freely roaming the taiga

wisteria and sunshine

the tide heaving and swelling

sand iced with colored shells

sun rays slanting into misty valleys

a beach of fine, sifted sand

the skeleton of a tree in winter

a slight peach tint in the orchard

black skimmers at a cape

swift trout streams in the hills

shrimp swimming backwards

a streusel of clouds

blue-in-the-shadows snow

a skeleton of a tree

clean water from a mountain-fed creek

the minuscule bumps on a strawberry

a completely still tree

a giant sugar pinecone

the bounty of the woods

a star against the night sky

fall colors in New England

calm before a storm

the spiraling of snowflakes

textured tree trunks

the smell of snow at night

Galapagos tortoises

the underside of a starfish

English peas or garden peas

the northward voyage of the sun

the way a whooping crane seeks home

multicolored rocky cliffs and slopes

the sky curdling at 4 p.m.

a vivid toucan in the wild

emus bobbing up and down

fresh flowering plants

birds watching bird-watchers

the white and granite gray of peaks

a light haze building at the horizon

billy goats bleating

rare prairie butterflies

shells in white sand

orangutans and siamangs of Indonesia

brightly hued bougainvillea

frost on the pumpkin

bats turning left when exiting a cave

berries ripe for the picking

prairie dogs on the lookout

pincushion protea flowers

bears hitching rides on ice floes

fallen pine needles

soft belly hair on goats

sand dunes at night

a bird convention in a tree

the cumuli in a June afternoon sky

a pleasure in pathless woods

the beach at night

new growth on the ends of branches

sky the color of graphite pencils

islands of seabird colonies

the bird chirping of spring

a sandstorm in the desert

spruce shaggy with usnea (lichens)

golden eagles cruising the skies

mini shelters for wintering birds

the dominance of nature over man

a squirrel-bird kerfuffle

giant water lilies

a recently formed fault scarp

osprey fattening up before nest-building

the cheerfulness of flowers

cattails, sea grape, bearberry

oysters changing gender

the ascent of sap in trees

cantaloupe warmed in the sun

the natural world, a library of ideas

dragonfruit from cacti

horticultural meditation

acres of seed heads

trees covered with icicles

the flat eyes of a Gila monster

endless green steppes

huge Patagonian hares

the tawny, dusty grass of summer

the naturally meditative state of cats

winter geese barking in the sky

barrier reef and salt marshes

the air smelling green

thickets of thorny scrub

pink flowers, pink sky

green trees after a spring rain

a plum tree spreading its wings

farmers beginning to work the fields

the real artist, Mother Nature

feathery goldenrod in vacant pastures

a full moon reflected on water

blue whales off California

a glimpse of an elusive bird

multicolored pebbles at the shoreline

seashells from last summer

fragrant balsams whispering

trees shaped by prevailing winds

when there's a blue sky

natural-sound recordings

mountaintops high as the jet stream

music in the roar of the deep sea

the remains of squirrel lunches

a polka-dot cowrie

Earth's envelope

the phases of the moon

a copper butterfly

a pink-beaches island

the ever-changing sky

a deeply fissured ice field

changes in natural light

the full Sturgeon Moon

tree roots extending

the cooing of a dove

the roar of a waterfall

a porcupine floating in water

crocus poking up out of the snow

the day young and damp with dew

pink French tulips

sun pouring light over stones

a dog's tail in neutral

a sunrise walk through the woods

wind cuffing the chill water

duck tracks in the sand

night owls fleeing the cottonwood

the life of a wave

the wine-purple of elm

a block of granite

the smell of fall in the air

full-blown pink blooms

bees charging the blossoms

the smell of an evergreen tree

masses of wild mushrooms after a rain

parallel linear dunes

canicular days, the dog days of summer

tranquil horse pasture

the earth, smelling of mushrooms

a lazy leaf caught on a breeze

the moon's light being reflected sunlight

a chorus sung by the wind

the flowers of the Mimosa shrub

fish jumping to catch insects

animal courtship and mating habits

this terraqueous globe

pinks and purples low on the horizon

the life of a tree

forests of rhododendron

a feeling of snow in the freezing air

the rupturing front of a glacier

a small puddle—a flodge

a bird-nesting refuge

large ammonite fossils

cascades of refreshing tropical rain

fog purring through the streets

peppermint starfish on a coral reef

mountains on a clear morning

a fox curling into a ball

a beautiful sunset over the mountains

birds at their feather work

a nuisance of cats

excited sounds of nature

otters and abalone

birds that fly by night

a glacial outwash plain

birds returning in clamorous flocks

a giant panda cub playing in a tree

the curve of a tortoise shell

deer swimming in the lake

compound eyes of butterflies

the night sky, serene

a field full of ripe pumpkins

the cloud-mottled sky

where herds of shaggy buffalo roam

range maps for birds

Arizona's giant cactuses

a daily sunset-watching ritual

the fragrance of new leaves

random stuff woven into a bird's nest

the tendril of an old vine

desert sage growing in rocky crags

dramatic 200-foot bluffs

puffins fishing for their supper

fields brooding, wild, abandoned

the dark whisper of a hemlock grove

musty huckleberry bushes

grapes grown in rich volcanic soil

a never-summer wilderness

the orbits of planets

flowers in crannied walls

a feast of panoramic vistas

squirrels looking for snacks

an oak leaf in autumn

a walkers' and bird-watchers' paradise

a meandering stream

grapes sparkling on the vine

a carpet of flowers on a forest floor

a rough and stormy coast

being outside at sunset

a wren's exuberant trill and liquid song

the cavernous green of aged leaves

tiny snails among blades of grass

a delicious warmth in the breeze

the sun, fat and powerful

pyrite and tourmalines

owls hooting and spooky sounds

the wings of a hovering bird

alpine scenery and flora

the texture of lemon peel

the faces of pansies

an educational public garden

a fox den in the side of a hill

baby horses whinnying a coloratura

a leaden gray ocean

blue canyons in the sky

crickets' and cicadas' shrill songs

snowy beaches and billowy palms

pansies' velvety, innocent faces

left-handed polar bears

the keel-billed toucan

surf sweeping across your toes

velvet-black infinite sky

a nest of baby birds

the shine of wet leaves

our beautiful little planet

a deep purple velvet sky

turquoise containing traces of copper

the buzzy trill of the lorikeet

whales spouting off the headlands

the sky turning opalescent

an elephant trumpeting

the frowning brow of the lion

an uncleared forest

a goldfinch couple foraging

the pale new growth on an evergreen

sea beginning to surge into a wave

pineapples with their prickly skins

a cloudy day after many sunny days

the shades of the sky

a vivid sunset on the beach

an empty desert resembling moonscape

delicious autumn, the mellower season

the bellow of a bull

ants scurrying among roots

a glacier-fed turquoise lake

an oyster shell opening

natural rock pools

rushes on the edge of a river bank

cotton-candy skies

the color of a dark, stormy sea

the smallest mammal, the bumblebee bat

a trail to explore or a hill to climb

the intensity of migrating birds

an emerald-green landscape

the smell of trees

copper butterflies

an area of outstanding natural beauty

driftwood on the shore

birds washing in a birdbath

the neck of a hummingbird

purple mophead hydrangeas

dolphins making faces

a lemur on a bamboo tree

Tuscan evergreen cypress

cool climates with snow

millions of herring spawning

the garden in winter

the continent's craton

snow clinging to spiderweb threads

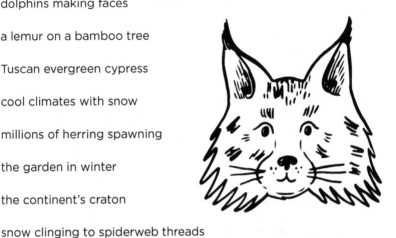

the early sun defining the sea

new leaves unfolding

moonlight and stars

lobsters the color of red lead

grain ripening to nuggets

air redolent with warm rain

hollyhock seedpods

rainbows shimmering over a river

the way rose petals fit together

a nutrient-laden farm pond

the rustle of ripened heads of wheat

spiders playing hide-and-seek

the leaves finally starting to change

the fall migration of whooping cranes

great soughing branches

a snowflake's slow, peaceful descent

pines stretching their arms

quiet woodland nooks

waves salty infoldings and outfoldings

an electrically green countryside

pink roses and white daisies

barren moonscapes of dark rock

birds hanging together in a tree

non-hybrid open-pollinated seeds

a single wild strawberry

the smell of wet stones

the wind whispering in your ears

an island with blueberry bushes

crazy bird chirping in a thicket

a swan drifting on a blackish river

a great desert cat, prowling

the canopy of a rain forest

the Eurasian steppe

the rapidity with which grass grows

a tree bent and twisted by fate

a moose in the wild

the sight of clouds from above

a bouquet of flowers you grew

the ivory-billed woodpecker

the zebra finch song

fresh, salty ocean and wet sand

brambles thick and impenetrable

flakes of snow falling slowly on you

a giant one-armed saguaro

a cold frame for tender plants

the smell of sunflowers

ospreys nesting in tall pines

a wave hanging and then breaking apart

the magnificence of the ocean

huge sprays of bamboo shoots

an iguana holding its breath

a cool overcast day

the gold around the frog's eyes

a cactus in winter

sand dunes' colors

a crash of lightning

an oak ruched with lichen

a cat watching bunnies outside

gigantic tree ferns

the swash zone of a beach

tree trunk variations

the conversations of birds

sunlight after a storm

foam chasing up the beach

the dusky glow of sunset

peaches and apricots

seahorses linking tails

bush hyrax and rock hyrax families

gardens with a perennial border

a high-spirited thoroughbred

the bleating of lambs

color after a gray winter

the solitary fluting of a wood thrush

an eagle soaring above a canyon

a sudden carpet of snow

the scent of a wisteria canopy

monogamous spoonbills

the arrangement of the stars

gardens grown by children

desert plants with very long roots

a lone eagle, soaring

flower-rich margins at field edges

dewy grass underfoot

birds bathing in a fountain

a full-blown red rose

graphite's silvery grit

sea air, lucid and pungent

cormorants and sea stacks

branches laden with fruit

the whirl of last fall's leaves

crane flies

a powdering of stars

moonlight in the pines

reflections on a blue lake

the solitude of a treetop

red and pink roses

an uncharted island

glorious countryside

an evergreen forest

the great blue heron

honeybees rushing flower to flower

curlews skipping along the beach

the slow step of a white heron

channels traced for rivers

the sun devouring all shadow

lilac and forsythia bushes

the chemical formula of a rose's scent

spectacular maple leaves

the stalk end of a tomato

cacti blooming in the desert

the distinctly vernal clamor of birds

mountain goats in the snow

a storm of falling leaves

the chitter of squirrels

waves slapping against rocky coves

oxen resting while standing

Antarctic Sound at sunset

maples donning fall coats

the blue of evening

water droplets shimmering on plants

the discovery of other solar systems

an extremely green grasshopper

blooms coming full cycle

foxes digging burrows, called earths or dens

open meadows and a brook meandering

a shell found along the beach

cormorants racing down the coast

raccoons raiding a sweet corn patch

bees disappearing into the hive

plants drinking water

bitterroot petals pink as taffy

horses flicking their tails

rare specimen trees

the ripples of a swirling stream

mangrove-fringed river branches

a rainbow after a sun shower

morsels of sweet delight on bushes

tiny yellow blades of seagrass

the cycle of the seasons

the whorls of a snail shell

a fin cutting through water

the smell of the skin of an orange

a garden sparkling after a shower

dunes appearing opalescent at sunrise

potted herbs for windowsill growing

baby red pandas in the Himalayas

a tree with spread-out branches

early morning thunderstorms

clouds materializing, clouds dancing

the day after an autumn storm

red silk pears from Oregon

the sea's pelagic region

a beautifully conical mountain peak

a frog napping in tulip petals

the scent of persimmon

a mockingbird's song repertoire

fruit trees at bud break

sandstone mountains

a salt marsh's inhabitants

a collection of seashells

how new leaves arrange themselves

a dolphin's dorsal fin

raindrops falling—*tink, tink*

the pageant of the changing seasons

leaves tumbling over empty hills

a glacier cascading into the sea

a whiff of gardenia

a deep green Irish lough

the fragrance of meadows and heaths

the dizzying smell of fresh-cut hay

phantom rain in a desert

luxurious green mosses

ducks gliding on a pond

minute ostrich feathers

squadrons of clouds above a forest

a sandstone slot canyon

an albino squirrel

winter on a windy beach

fall overtaking summer

multicolored rocks

the churning water of big rivers

an arctic air mass

leaves bursting from their buds

a troop of warthogs on the run

companion planting

a sea otter mother and newborn pup

hidden springs discovered

fields of peat and cut grass

wild cats at night

a show of birds in a formation flight

that giraffes make almost no sound

a landscape of pine and red clay dirt

autumn-fat squirrels, digging

barley growing tall and plump

the oldest known mineral, zircon

the plumes of the pine

graupel, granular snow pellets

the forces of nature

in winter, breathing in sea smell

the earth as an ever-changing stage

a meadow of wild grasses

the buttery flesh of a Hass avocado

a wild profusion of tomatoes

a record low at the peak of summer

the first robin in the spring

bees buzzing and making honey

the most beautiful cat in the world

the sweet motion of leaves

red, orange, and yellow dahlias

a school of whales swimming by

deer wandering the woodland

fog lathering up a stubby field

a long wave moving steadily shoreward

a spot where sunsets look otherworldly

the Gulf Stream current

snow lying serenely

koalas having unique fingerprints

wind undulating on mossy hills

worms after a rain

brooks beginning to burble

the blue of chicory flowers

a little thicket quivering with life

the autumnal gold of a salt marsh

branches of cottonwoods encased in ice

the air turning colder

a squirrel running along a fence

bright green celery

balsam-scented air

bunny rabbit visitors

the wind blowing over prairie grasses

the quiet after a thunderstorm ends

animals when they escape their enemies

hammerhead sharks massing together

gray squirrels chattering

wheat turning the color of molten gold

fish gliding through the deep, dark sea

a squirrel's change of mind/direction

plants greening out

wheat rippling in the wind

bare branches etched in the moonlight

birds sinking into the sky

the trill of the tree sparrow

the air turning cool, then moist

a marsh full of cattails

heart-shaped anthuriums

sunshine after days of rain

patches of briers and blackberries

the limitless and lonesome prairie

a river giggling in secret amusement

a soft-tinted desert

green tussocked fields

brown branches clotted with ice

dawns rimmed with silver frost

the white full moon of midsummer

dramatic and panoramic landscapes

the pinkish bloom of daybreak

soft beds of fresh pine needles

a wooded grove at the lap of the sea

turtles sliding into the water

the chatter of a squirrel

the raving of crows

durum wheat fields

sugarbush, a stand of maple trees

the gold-soaked mists of autumn

a tortoise taking its time

a pinecone bird feeder

turquoise blue skies

acorns—the bread of the woods

a shimmering moonlit waterfall

twilights in autumn

robins on the lawn

variegated holly leaves

agate geode crystals

a pink-and-blue-striped sunrise

evergreens bearded with snow

a large group of laughing gulls

a wave rising slowly, then briskly

the Indian elephant

a clump of violets growing alone

the texture of eggshells

foxes running by, unconcerned

the chilly skies of a northern winter

birds navigating by starlight

pretty flowers growing by a brick wall

grass and sedge spikelets

cow tails swinging

the scent of vineyard grapes

cool, moss-covered paths

Denali, an orogeny in progress

pandas lolling luxuriously in the sun

the many shapes of leaves

flowers opening overnight

the purity of a mountaintop scene

variegated colors in an agate's bands

the smell of thyme in the fields

Mount Everest growing every year

the sky portending a cold front

all the complexions of bark

a spiderweb's silvery flash of dew

a wooded promontory

dolphins cruising the creeks and bays

a patter of nuts falling from trees

cattails frozen in the snow

a cat watching a bug

pumpkins spilling from the patch

gray perambulations of cloud patterns

the pohutukawa plant of New Zealand

four splendid seasons

the fading light of winter sunset

how wild birds' songs evolve

exotic flamingo flowers and caladiums

aimless walks down empty footpaths

fresh noon sunlight

white-tailed deer in the clearing

the near and far sides of the moon

the garden at dusk

underground streams

a tall tree whose growth is interior

sun glittering in the waves

a teeming, noisy bird sanctuary

nature's conspiracy to keep us happy

the filmy veils of morning

powder-blue mountains

bioluminescence of living creatures

the blossoming moors and orchards

the whisper of pine trees in the wind

lavender wafting through the air

skates' eggs on the sand

the feel of a frog in your hand

stars you can almost touch

moonlight seeping into rooms

jaybirds drunk on chinaberries

a rising star at sunset

a geological work of art

the beauty of a giraffe at sunset

a winding trail beside a musical brook

the astonishing blue of a mountain sky

tall daisies and luxuriant grasses

an array of hedgehogs

a beech forest covered in hoarfrost

the seed pod of a lotus flower

a whiff of fresh mountain air

fresh breezes in the evening

heart-shaped pebbles and rocks

a birdwatchers' path

three-pronged webbed tracks

archaeological ruins lying hidden in a forest

white and lemon lichen blotches

the afternoon shade of the apple tree

dandelions that have gone to seed

a flurry of juncos defying the wind

a group of giraffes

snow on the evergreens

sharks you can swim with

beans beginning to pod

that the nature of nature is healing

unfallen rain in the air

seeds cast to the wind

a no-visibility snow squall

the fossilized remains of a fern

worms crawling through the damp earth

Atlantic white-sided dolphins

gray squirrels in white aprons

a watch of nightingales

stands of golden cordgrass

a cascade of aromatic roses

wildlife near your house

saguaros at sunset

man and nature working in harmony

the fiery sun setting over the sea

cubs: bear, fox, lion, tiger

the smell of marigolds

ice formations on a gurgling spring

the tributary flowing into the lake

an exquisite work of nature

embankments lined with weeping willows

worms busy turning leftovers into soil

a bright winter's afternoon

a deeply sheltered mountain lake

an ice wall at the front of a glacier

a bobcat's stubby tail

the breeze in the trees

a light dusting of snow

the great wildebeest migration

an old weeping willow washing her hair

Flemish giant rabbits

a big cloud blocking the hot sun

raindrops on brown leaves

a garden glowing, backlit by the sun

a tiny clump of snow

the edge of a river, lake, or ocean

the sound of river rapids

maples turning a blazing red

gulls riding the breezes

a seashell whispering into the ear

pointed mountain peaks

enormous pumpkins and squashes

animal-specific vocals

the color of a Maine summer sky

beaches loud with heavy surf

animals living unobserved lives

the color of daffodils

a vug, a small cavity in a rock

frost-covered trees looking like cotton balls

an ambience to outdoor light

large peaceful fields

rugged mist-covered mountains

platinum-colored wheat grass

the color of claret cup cactus

a bird flying into the clouds

trees' network with other trees

polar bears passing through

fresh flowers on the kitchen table

red-tailed hawks' magnificent screams

leaves budding on trees

the height of clouds

live oaks draped with Spanish moss

leaves doing whatever the wind demands

rocks eroded by rivers

the tea olive's intense sweetness

peach trees in bloom

a picnic lunch in a blueberry patch

cats polishing people's ankles

the fading scent of autumn roses

a mountain in the far distance

a lion turning a shaggy head

the quiet part of the woods

ice towers on a glacier

indecently plump vine tomatoes

a tiny snail sitting on a daylily leaf

the stillness of early-morning fog

bright white clouds

the arms of an octopus

a forest floor full of butterweed

lemon-scented gum trees

a forest of mixed hardwoods or pines

beans arching through the soil

animal collective names

grape or bubble coral

little silver fish darting by

new plants for the garden

flowers following the sun

Vs of migrating birds

the strange zoophyte

a garden still flourishing in autumn

the meadow vole in its cave

air filled with shimmering snowflakes

stony coves full of shorebirds

isopods' seven pairs of legs

raspberries and violets

the markings of an owl

the leafy caverns of summer

a baby bunny (a kitten) with its mommy

wind blowing through a forest of ice

a flower buffet for insects

spray blown up from wave tops

a little bird's whisper

the thunder of waves

a cat's total relaxation

the bullfrog, who never sleeps

fog bending the light in the morning

the dendrites of a snowflake

when wind meets mountains

a cottonwood bursting into leaf

wood drakes resting on the water

the wild starscape above a desert

crystalline polar sea

eggs in camouflaged nests

the hollow rapping of a woodpecker

a bloat of hippopotami

acres of awe-inspiring greenery

burnt orange chrysanthemums

the freckles of a tiger

snails and crabs seeking shelter

a perturbed porcupine

how a bird teaches a chick to fly

animal rescue groups

original stands of timber

in winter, waking up to snow

turtles sitting on logs

a male seahorse giving birth

buttercups and columbines

cumulus clouds over fireweed

enormous golden moons

the golds and reds of autumn

old rocks casting long shadows

the grace of a dolphin

red berries on a big evergreen tree

luminescent plankton

a placid lakeshore

rain ending a drought

sunlight-infused woods

easy walks in pine forests

the power of the Atlantic and Pacific

the patterns of ocean currents

houseplants' air-cleaning ability

golden exhalations of the dawn

patterns in nature

a pandemonium of parrots

the silent world underwater

roses in full riotous bloom

baby marsupials sleeping

moon glowing through the fog

a classic Cape Cod seascape

the endless permutations of snowflakes

birches lithe as dancers

all the colors of sea on a cloudy day

ice forts' milky blue shadows

snow monkeys taking a sauna

the intricateness of snake's scales

clouds playing charades

the first orange flower of autumn

rain putting you to sleep

the 75 miles of Earth's atmosphere

irises of every shade

snow in the mountains

an extensive organic garden

termites' caste systems

the weightlessness of snow

the smell of damp earth

snow trickling down the skin of a tree

a butterfly's 12,000 eyes

lupines and poppies by the acre

lazy waves on the beach

nature's vibrant spectrum

geological deposit layers

falcons flying across the ground

the rain singing you a lullaby

summer's scorching glow

a walk through a botanical garden

strong, tough, fearless winter gulls

pink-blossomed peach trees

a clearing in the forest

Iceland's Blue Lagoon

the world in a grain of sand

an osprey drifting on a thermal

sunlight slanting through junipers

ponds glazed with ice

hairs on a sunflower bud

a heavily glaciated, active volcano

light flowing through tree branches

a bird chirping happily

limbs of trees covered with snowflakes

a breeze with flower scents

smooth pebbles shimmering on the beach

tiny dogs that walk really fast

the Everglades wilderness

proboscis monkeys in dense jungles

frost-heaved rubble called felsenmeer

an ancient ilex tree

waterfalls cascading from rock spires

nature as the soundtrack

a squirrel leaping among the arbors

the way chipmunks move

visits from a little-seen animal

the hanging nest of an oriole

the 36,000 quills of a porcupine

a dose of wilderness therapy

the teeming floor of a rain forest

an unexpected sunny day

mossy hiking trails

a faint flow painting the horizon

a brook falling from rock to rock

fragrant fields and forests

all the corn in Kansas

pinecones littering the trail

the quiet of sundown

water crashing on a sea wall

a murky lagoon full of water birds

ice palaces in windswept rookeries

mid-oceanic ridges

sunlight streaming through the trees

sapphire, clear, forest-lined lakes

wild turkeys perched on trees

a well-behaved honeybee

a mockingbird dancing in the air

pine trees' recipe for renewal

life cycles found in nature

the beauty and geometry of a pinecone

turquoise and yellow songbirds

the Pacific Northwest rain forest

fences covered with honeysuckle

signs of a new season emerging

a 100-foot-tall banyan tree

aerial photos of fall foliage

birds looking for natural food

the changing scenes along a shore

an island of nature in an urban sea

the megamouth shark

bunches of ducks swimming in water

the arctic fox and wolf

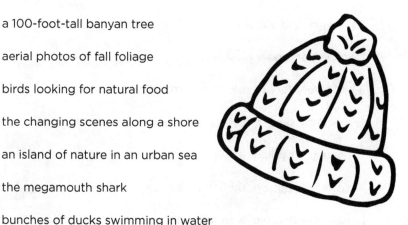

shorebirds chasing the tide

the final glow of sunset

checkerspot butterflies

the mindful meditation of trails

roses straggling over a fence

large ripples in the shallow ocean

asters as big as saucers

the sunward side of a tree

a patch of sunlight on a distant hill

alfalfa and onion sprouts

seeds that have wings

uncut rain forests

bats swarming out of a cave

foxgloves and pear blossoms

a bird's very funny walk across a roof

Old Faithful geyser, Wyoming

the sunspot cycle of about 11 years

a glacier's tongue gathering up stones

blue jays fluffed big as ruffed grouse

vineyards clinging to hillsides

whitened sand dollars

aardvarks snacking on ants

crocodiles galloping

a penguin with its baby on its feet

the powdery sands of the Sahara

a playa, a dried-up lake bed

sunrise on the beach or shore

fickle spring weather

the frosted meadow

a scattering of fragrant balsam trees

the social hierarchy of birds

dicentra (bleeding heart) plants

icy crystals of queenly snowflakes

otters' whiskers and dark fur

monk seals at play

baby sparrows hopping

leaf buds on the trees

the forest morning

Niagara Falls in full flow

bright yellow ginkgoes

a coastal fog belt

Azov, the world's shallowest sea

whimsical mountain winds

the roar of a tidal wave

bubbles in a stream

a granite shoreline sheathed in ice

clear days after a storm

the aroma of approaching winter

a reflection of the sky in a puddle

the formation of an island

brittle leaves on trees

the classical elegance of calla lilies

gingerly stepping through a garden

the frosty surface of a silent lake

southern fox squirrels

icicles dripping and melting

burdock seed heads and bindweed

a cold spring downpour

a garden adorned in nature's ornaments

chinstrap penguins

days hot enough to ripen tomatoes

the feel of the wind on your cheeks

a huge expanse of prairie

a memento from nature

the windrow-drift of weeds and shells

animals calling their mates

gnarled sunflower leaves

June dewdrops spangling phlox

the autumnal equinox

clouds chasing each other

a lakefront you went to as a child

a spring day in the 50s

an aerial view of a peach orchard

the spitting furnace of the sun

pecan-colored light at dawn

pines rustling agreeably in the breeze

the balance of nature

the blush of sunrise

a brown bear catching a leaping salmon

nature's peace flowing into you

the resilience of a turtle

goldenrod tossing on the wind

strings of pahoehoe (ropy lava)

birches bowing in the wind

the sound of a raccoon

a tranquil sunny haze

the morning after the first frost

hexagonal snow crystals

an owl under the maple tree

the top of the Himalayas

a lemon cypress plant

trees admiring their long shadows

swans elegantly floating

a hike-and-bike trail

birds riding the thermals

aphids and ladybugs

an icy rushing river

a dark golden bee hovering and humming

sunrise after a snowfall

bright frosty mornings

ephemeral frangipani blossoms

the scent of citrus

extremes of nature reconciled

weeds yellowed in the first frost

a pebble that looks as good dry as wet

the belly of a Beluga whale

heavy rain with big drops

an indigo bunting on a sunflower

squirrels chattering on a limb

gelatinous rain right before sleet

a hundred birds in a single tree

tracks of snowbirds

new shoots on a plant

the Cretaceous and Tertiary periods

a skink rising from its bog

sea cows or manatees

a scavenging of seagulls

cicadas in full voice

redwoods getting water from fog

a gray day at sunset

orange sugar maple trees

a chickadee calling from a birdhouse

cedar tree resilience

mosses trailing under the water

a bed of clams or oysters

orange trees' profusion of blossoms

a bird's contour feathers

puzzling sounds in nature

the whiteness of a whale

butterflies matching the flowers

the kick of a vanishing rodent

mountains still growing

the beautiful breezes of autumn

underwater animal life

swallows' annual mud nests

the winter plum blossom

the calving of Greenland ice

lava flowing slowly

a beautiful meadow with no bugs

geese talking to each other

sunset through the trees

the distant whoop of a spotted hyena

trout visible through clear waters

the magnitude of a star

a snow-dusted winter paradise

full-grown pumpkins in the garden

downy woodpeckers and nuthatches

a shaft of light from a nearby star

the layers of a geological deposit

the smell of a forest

squid eyes, the size of watermelons

an active geyser in Iceland

the fellowship of dawn and dusk

the supple stems of fresh Amaranthus

grass dressed with dewfall

the colors of sunrise

wildlife preserves

chestnut trees along a river

cool ocean breezes

the vivid yellow of rapeseed blossoms

dappled sunlight patterns

small waves lisping on the sand

the color of wheat

the wind changing at night

a garden in all its moods

zephyr, a breeze from the west

fields of lavender and olive trees

bicolor red and yellow tulips

snow sparkling in the sunlight

a seal sliding into the water

a great hemlock forest

the sun disappearing behind a hill

a rare shell from the ocean floor

winter moon, bright stars

the top of a windswept hill

migration patterns of birds

an underground sea of lava

the feathery top of a dandelion

firebrick sea stars

a laughing gull scooting by the shore

Earth's only edible rock, salt

the sound of ice and snow melting

a just-born baby hippo

great winds across the sky

no two snowflakes being alike

insects at play, outside

the sunsets of autumn and winter

rain falling on prepared soil

the center of the earth

a whiff of fragrant flowers

the nose leaf on bats

the long sliding song of a nightingale

a hot spring with orange algae fringe

the salt smell of shore breezes

a little egg laying on a leaf

school classes held in the woods

squirrels fattening up

a languid river in the noonday sun

fog from melting snow

crickets hearing in ultrasound

the birds and bees

squirrels growing fluffy bellies

a beaver paddling through a stream

barren strawberry in the short grass

the nuances of dawn

winter bird-watching

white phlox tossing and thrashing

birds singing in the bushes

an obstinacy of buffalo

a fertile river valley

the first patters of rain

the rising energy of the waxing moon

a rabbit's home under a tree

shades of a country morning

fresh air after being stuck indoors

evergreen softwoods, peaceful meadows

the inside of a cat's ears

a cacophony of animal noises

the sea grinding down rock

a little gleaming river

the ocean post-sunset

frost flowers on a window

a crater caused by a meteor

the overarching laws of nature

the whispers of the trees

Venus looking at Mars

a first-taste-of-winter storm

the darkness and coolness of a cave

skimmers catching fish

a rainbow filling the sky with color

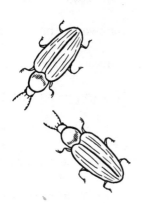

wavelike patterns in the sand

rain, falling sluggishly

a snowhole dug as temporary shelter

geese in a wishbone formation

the chattering of birds

an osprey eating a fish dinner

vines clambering up the walls

ladybugs on aphid duty

grass growing extra green and juicy

the last of the snow melting

the speed of the sei whale

marshy pastures where hawks hunt

bowers of honeysuckle

autumn's sun-ripened fruits

deep-green Swiss chard

the screech of an owl

the angle of a bird's wing

bright green buds on the trees

a dragonfly hovering

how a bird suspends itself in the air

a maritime fog forest

a cygnet on the lake

wind combing blades of grass

animals filling ecological niches

when spring is delayed

a riot of wildflowers

impact craters found on Earth

an alligator in the wild

a butterfly pavilion

when a plant grows and grows

daisies reflected in dewdrops

varied growth patterns in trees

the undulating outline of hills

the plumeless genus of bipeds

soft smooth beaches

moss spreading at the base of an oak

leaves bursting with color

the hard blue ice of a northern lake

the resiliency of wildflowers

icebergs of an improbable powder blue

snowfall in a steep mountain gorge

a sunrise bike ride or hike

the external features of a butterfly

pink light arriving in the marshes

sun hitting colored treetops

aspen leaves shivering

a bird fussing over her nest

bees sipping the roses

bamboo that is 150 feet tall

the vast silence of Antarctica

rockhopper penguins

the food and oxygen we get from plants

the clear hyaline, the glassy sea

sun baking through the soil

early corn beginning to tassel out

the patience of animals

the flowers in the garden

Japanese maple trees

lily pads floating on a pond

the fauna of a small habitat

tranquil landscapes

sweet chestnut's bark

post-thunderstorm earth smell

the strength of a spiderweb

the bumpiness of an orange peel

Niagara Falls frozen solid

a tree in a pearly cloud of mistletoe

fat iridescent pigeons

trees starting to get dressed

amber mountains and blazing gardens

woods filled with golden sundrops

the oak, a dominant monolith

the sound of a woodland stream

a moonscape plateau between two peaks

glimpses of small secret gardens

the quiet breathing of night

lots of green underfoot

foam dissolving as waves recede

the details of an autumn leaf

flowers' short, beatific lives

red-rimmed sandstone bluffs

vertiginous cliffs

large, bushy hydrangeas

a perfect hybrid tea rose

the twiggy end of branches

bare feet on soft moss

the way air feels before a storm

a vermilion shovelfish

the shade of an old tree

a full lunar eclipse

the highly developed crocodile brain

woodpeckers foraging

a beaver tail slap

the smell of really, really clean air

an ice sheet booming like a giant drum

the colors in a brilliant autumn leaf

the calipash and calipee of a turtle

low-bush blueberries on rock cairns

a thunderstorm to cool the air

birds hunting for seeds

an unexpected rainbow

the sound of spring frogs and crickets

nature choosing the moment of birth

fragrant carpets of wild thyme

the poetry in all natural things

daffodil bulbs

submarine mountain ranges

the brilliance of a new moon

heavy purple cones of fragrant lilac

pebbles washed down from a mountain

a splendid glistening black stallion

the shape of a cat paw

soft, mist-hung green meadows

a red rock arch on a beach

a macaque swinging from limb to limb

boulders carried here by glaciers

clouds gradually uncovering the moon

volcanic deposits containing iron

rainbows and snowdrops

sunshine on your face

a hundred acres of tideland

the snap of icicles thawing

hermit crabs running

branches closing overhead

hybrid daylilies, Resurrection lilies

the earthworm digging its tunnels

the first flower to bloom every year

daybreak in the woods

donkeys in the wild

long cloud fingers combing the sky

day gladly alternating with night

the roar of a creek

the sound of blackbird wings

cloud plumes rising

the sound of a body of water

a rock-ribbed coast

Monarch butterflies migrating south

a pink amaryllis blooming

an oxpecker on a hippo

silver salmon runs

watermelon and cantaloupe fields

moss on an old stone wall

grass stitched to the ground

creatures that hunt at night

Earth rising above the lunar horizon

a worm emerging from the ground

waves skittering along the shoreline

a nest of wet stones on a beach

a wild garden basking in the sun

dead trees that still stand

oaks dripping with Spanish moss

eucalyptus salubris trees

small fields bordered by stone walls

the mysteries of Earth

sunlight buttering the landscape

birds singing at sunrise

landscape, the product of circumstance

your connection with wild nature

Darwin's finch on a giant tortoise

elderflowers, the flower of the elder

bright yellow-and-black damselfish

the life history of a typical star

trees beginning to wake up

loblolly pines near a spring

a robin's puffed-out chest

a long hike into the country

cornfields in late July

the Atlantic churning on rocks

wolf maples growing near stone fences

an oyster making a pearl

flower petals reaching to the sky

the tongue of a penguin

trees heavy-limbed with shining apples

the Alps seen from above

the camel, the pride of the desert

leafy enclaves and rocky riverbanks

animals as masters of touch

the tiptoe prints of deer

the crunch of leaves underfoot

beautifully changing foliage

winter sea, winter sun

visible meteor showers

the tranquilizing effects of sunlight

nature's bounteousness

the sweet smell of damp earth

surprise wildlife sightings

leaves decaying under bushes

shell-pink dog rose in high summer

cucumbers with silver-wired leaves

rowan or mountain ash

jellyfish moving through water

elms turning yellow, then rusting

bright pink crab apple trees blooming

the sun rising a ribbon at a time

lucky peach blossoms and kumquat trees

an outcrop of rock

a dusting of starlight

dawn's early light

the sun setting slowly

never-tilled tallgrass prairie

early spring breezes

nature's prerogatives

bluebells carpeting a forest floor

ocean water glistening

DNA's millions of atoms

the circular pattern of star trails

a bird's graceful landing

birds perched on wires

the rosy light of dawn

the steady thrum of the surf

shadows of the clouds

the restfulness of a flower garden

the stifle of a horse's hind leg

a rock fixed in the middle of a river

leaves shiny from rain

droop-eared doggies

the smell of water-soaked air

the rushing of spring runoff

afternoon light tinting the snow pink

each leaf on a plant

the sudden scent of pine pitch

house-size boulders

moon reflecting off the sea

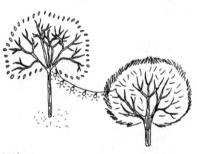

dwarf trees or arbuscles

worms in slow motion

leaves chasing each other in a circle

mesquite trees' deep roots

wind sanding things smooth

crocuses in all sorts of colors

trees growing in weird directions

a bird's slow ascent through the pines

a lovely pale moon

the tiny petals of the mountain ash

the brown carpet of last year's leaves

how a tree reacts to circumstance

the geoid that is the Earth

the stars and moon reflecting on water

snow falling on Christmas Eve

a partridge sitting on her eggs

blossoms tumbling by a pasture gate

the antics of chimpanzees

a butterfly alighting on a flower

the light between downpours

sea air swirling around you

the lonely howl of the wind

the way a beach looks at sunset

a trellised rose bed

the gray flux before spring

snow frosting on the fields

the garden's night shift

snow adding an extra layer of silence

the edge between dark and light

open summits with 360-degree views

grasshoppers thrashing in the brush

fossils bleached in sun and rain

brown hares in a boxing match

the light of stars on a clear night

sunflower seeds, each one a new life

a vast nature preserve

a plump pink starfish

lilac bushes twisted like cables

any time the seasons change

the earthquakes no one feels

the Arizona desert in spring

a starfish in the tide pools

a wave beginning to roll

nature taking over

the smell of flooded meadows

stone walls of New England granite

trees' patience, grass's persistence

rain that arrives after sundown

the spiritual power of an ancient tree

snow geese and sandhill cranes

a puddle of summer rain

the bumpy surface of Indian corn

the smooth, waxy surface of peppers

birds singing with no lessons

a dog that is not barking

saguaros, ocotillos, and chollas

the wonderful smell of hay and horses

how branching coral grows

rhodies in full bloom

the smell of salt air

long, golden surf beaches

moss and damp mulch

the whorls of a shell

a thistle flower and seed head

the golden eyes of snowy owls

fields beckoning to you

the Andromeda galaxy

a nodding sunflower

a cluster of scarlet milkweed

humpbacks gorging on anchovies

repeated rain squalls

an eggshell—white, fragile, unbroken

trails up nearby mountains

grooves and channels in sandstone

a fat bumblebee hovering

a glacier inching along

beautiful landlocked green fields

plum dahlias and tangerine roses

lazy afternoons by the sea

pink and blue skies

brightly colored coral

pollen motes in the air

the laws of planetary motion

miles of lonely, windblown beach

the moon's white spotlight

mountain goats scrambling rock to rock

a whale nudging the bow of a boat

a cross-island trail

rivers that steam and mud that boils

a playful family of river otters

a tree with a little wind in it

the majestic Indian peacock

the smooth shiny surface of a plum

illustrations of natural history

an undulating grassy steppe in summer

Mother Nature showing off

wind moaning in the pines

basil and tarragon perfuming the air

ravens' tracks in mud

buffaloes being good swimmers

the scrabbling of nocturnal creatures

a glimpse of a deer

the early nightfall of winter

branches with new growth

a tree in bloom/blossom

invisible night rain

last snow and first flowers

a peach that is sweet and fuzzy

swallows circling a house and barn

a moonless night in the desert

the face of a mandrill

a pond without green scum

ice glaze on a pond

flowers poking up through the soil

the Zen of cat breathing

trails without maps

the call of loons and ospreys

a wild sanctuary of rugged beauty

the sound of running water in a brook

summer scraping the heels of spring

resident birds of your area

water trickling into snowmelt

soft soapstone rock

cream-colored butterflies

the many color combos of pansies

an otter relaxing on its back

giant California pinecones

a wold—open, rolling hills

the fizz of hummingbirds

the moss upon the forest bank

a whitecoat, harp seal pup

the smell of sage in the hills

a river, cold, fresh, and alive

nature's raw materials

a falling star to wish upon

flowers that only open at night

the smoothness of a fresh egg

billows of spume bashing a seawall

pelicans clamoring for today's catch

a bouquet of peonies

the almost neon green of spring

a breathtaking garden

the whisper of summer rain

a blue-gray valley mist

super large snowflakes

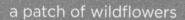
a patch of wildflowers

a coalition of cheetahs

Paleozoic metamorphic highlands

the scent of sweetbriar in the air

when the sea lions come out to play

hibiscus the size of trees

carrots sprouting in grassy lines

beautiful swans sitting on their nests

a parliament of owls

arrays of cloud parcels

a flax field

ladybugs in December

a bighorn materializing out of mist

night air stirring the leaves

willows by a slow river

giraffes cleaning their ears

a willow waving in the wind

apples tumbling from backyard trees

winter trees defrocked of leaves

an autumn tunnel of trees

a cloud upstaging a massive moon

the giant lily of the Amazon

wilderness to explore

crimson- and apricot-colored flowers

grizzly bears searching for berries

the immense quiet of empty country

daisies and buttercups and cloves

the fireproof bark of the redwood tree

a seal's breathing hole in the ice

the hollow mansions of the upper air

a shrimp's almost-transparent body

stars pinning the sky back

a white dove in pallid golden light

the light trickle of a stream

birds eating birdseed

strange mating rituals

a kingfisher's spark of color

the Pacific Crest Trail

a blizzard bringing drought relief

well-tended vegetable gardens

hawks hang-gliding over the desert

nighttime nature noises

emus and kangaroos

the sweet pulse of crickets

squirrels burying and hoarding nuts

geese herding their fluffy newborns

clouds' vague and beautiful faces

the monogamy of a mandarin duck

a rare albino deer

the dawn redwood, a deciduous tree

huge schools of tropical fish

a heifer in clover

the hummingbird's vibrating visit

bald eagles fishing

the bent trunk of a windblown tree

a low layer of lumpy clouds (stratus)

when a cicada stops making noise

the thin air at higher altitudes

natural bridges and arches

phlox, snapdragons, stocks, hollyhocks

the feel of the sun on your arms

sea otters holding hands

springtime in the Alps

wildflower-rich hay meadows

dramatic Rocky Mountain scenery

the rough shaggy bark of the pine

the morning clamor of birds

clear blue creek waters

the grace of a cat

a sunset behind the mountains

a late evening sky of changing pastels

tiny water beads on flower petals

the 35 basic types of snowflake

the changing Earth

an eagle in flight

pink sunlight on a lake

the Geminid meteor shower

a meltwater tunnel in a glacier

left-eye flounders

the uneven shoreline

a field of daisies

the exquisite monotony of bird calls

one last azalea bloom of the season

daffodil green emerging

the orange globe of citrus sun

petals slowly closing

rain on newly sprouted cornfields

bees' waggle dance

gently undulating countryside

heavily antlered elk

a windswept field of snow

air sweet and crisp as cider

the primal forces of nature

the ordered regularity of vines

waves coming in, then retreating

great egrets and red-winged blackbirds

a satisfying hike

mountains covered with a rug of trees

dark, gesticulating trees

pigs rolling around in the mud

the tonic of wilderness

the low music of birds, croodle

huge waves crashing on rocks

purple martins swooping for insects

the fragrance of white pine

a clutch of chicks

red autumnal leaves of sycamore

a softly rainy spring day

the low of kine heard along the meads

a bunny popping out of its burrow

the patience of a bear

the sun gradually using all its paints

a sweet and perfect winter silence

the lilac's first bloom

snow drifts to jump in

the nip of early winter

birds gathered in a treetop

gentle rain falling upon a lake

antlers poking out of hiding

a blue jay feather

tundra swans and snow geese

when it looks like a snow globe outside

a kaleidoscope butterfly bush

an ancient multihued mountain range

the canyons of Colorado

frost whitening the lawn

the lavender of twilight

a full moon and no clouds

a path of violets and daisies

an enchanted ladder of moonlight

sea turtles at night

bees and the flowers they pollinate

the thin crickets of midsummer

sanderlings sleeping on a beach

a puddle that freezes overnight

animal parents caring for babies

a sea turtle hatchling

gardens used for meditation

the shadow of a high-flying eagle

snow showers melting on touchdown

a paperbark maple's peeling bark

cairns of fist-sized rocks

countless desert sands

spectacular winter sunrises

the percussion of rain

growth rings of a tree

ranger talks at wildlife centers

the quarreling of nesting birds

a charm of goldfinches

rivers shaping the landscape

sea sheep (sea slugs)

the eyes of a small animal

an elephant squirting water

flowers dressed in light

cream-colored ponies

a balmy summer's eve

deep darkness, waves lapping

a tree at home in an unhomely place

brook sounds lacing the darkness

bats' sonar system

animal chit-chat by a stream

the curly coat of poodles

crimson dogwood in October

limestone cave systems

wind catching the leaves

a storm without wind

a close-up look at a hummingbird

raspy purple coneflowers

autumn's explosion of color

the meditation of beholding nature

frogs straying from ponds

snowflakes in lamplight

the first ladybug of spring

the smell of the earth in the woods

sweet Georgia peaches

wild turkeys strutting

the breath of life

the soft light of early evening

a total solar eclipse or lunar eclipse

the sight of an almond blossom

crinkly hawthorn leaves

jays raucous in the pines

whole foods, foods from nature

a snow crystal's six sides

tar sands and oil shales

a horseback ride through the hills

the date and time of the next eclipse

purple morning glory

the Perseid meteor shower

frosty blue sunrises in winter

when the maples turn

a beautiful crimson velvety berry

critters rustling in the ivy

herb beds laid out on three levels

acres of flowering bulbs

the animal and plant kingdoms

the sun, the world's best alarm clock

seals on a sandbar

musk mallow and musk roses

an elephant's huge, soft feet

mauve redbud trees

the bark of a rainbow eucalyptus tree

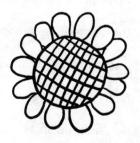

the motionless leaves of the scrub oak

a dandelion just before the wind blows

the color of the sky and deep sea

a distant sandy shore

a beautiful public garden

the sounds of a palm forest

a strange, isolated mountain

the sky at twilight

a marsh dominated by phragmites

the last day of summer

a canvas of flaming color in the fall

worms' survival during winter

metropolises of penguins

the powerful soughing of the sea

a stunning yellow spike of goldenrod

fields lambs have nibbled

wild radish plants

a dog's passion for sniffing

horses dozing broadside

the chalk cliffs of Dover

basilisk lizards running on water

flowers with a long flowering period

the earthy smell of mulch

beaks drinking the air

cypress's wide fluted bases

a snowdrop in bloom

species of marine life

a leaf bud, a gemma

horses sleeping standing up

the dunes at sunset

immense forests of chestnut trees

eels lying in wait among the rocks

the sound of a waterfall

swamp maples as scarlet as tanagers

the acacia-freckled African savanna

birds calling to each other

horses frolicking in the pasture

baby animals wrestling

the whirr of birds in flight, skirr

the pink-purple bloom of a ripe peach

wildlife following its own pattern

a rainbow of wildflowers

livestock cropping vegetation

a mountain in the sea

the first picnic of spring

snapdragons and camellias

the first frog quaver from the marsh

the speed of a dragonfly

the wind chime of leaves

violets after rain

cumulostratus clouds

nature not doing anything uselessly

a startling mushroom

Uranus's celestial shades of blue

lawns layered with crisp leaves

the pace of nature

fall berries in plump clusters

the smoke signals of the morning mist

quahogs, cherrystones, littlenecks

a meltwater lake on an iceberg

the power-roar of the sea

Hawaii's fascinating geology

the green bit of a carrot

fences of living plants

planet Earth as a giant magnet

the riches of the woods

lambs grazing in seaside pastures

pingo or frost mounds in permafrost

a very high island mountain

pink-and-blue-striped sunsets

the surface of a lake

big windows that look out on nature

life in estuaries

a bunny hunkered down in the grass

a long stretch of snowfields

the return of the swallows

the spray or splash zone of the ocean

pansies and primroses

miles of gentle nature trails

Arbor Day, for planting trees

the piping of marmots

field notes on nature

the texture of a tiger's coat

a pig snouting truffles

the blossom end of a banana

a confluence of two glaciers

a tidal pool after a wave has receded

dance displays by birds of paradise

the color of tree bark

mountains looking out at creation

the mood of a sacred cave

lush rice paddies

the sound of waves and hovering gulls

fritillary butterflies

swans singing as they fly

the structure of the atom

an altocumulus mackerel sky

a disarmingly calm ocean

pignut hickory trees

rain watering seedlings

the lava bubbling from the earth

the sound of horse hooves

clamorous bird flocks

cornstalks stretching skyward

river water twisting under moonlight

a mama giraffe kissing her baby

pink and yellow carnations

nature providing places to go barefoot

the smell of a lilac bush

rabbits sniffing potential food

bushy patches of catnip

deer growing new antlers

geese nipping food with short jerks

the beaver's camp

a lush lemon grove

icebergs drifting by

a tree growing from the inside

a leaf tossed by the wind

the quiet wisdom of nature

the fidget of bugs

grasses bowing in homage to the wind

a wild storm's pulse-revving intensity

the splash of a beaver

the new moon rising at sunrise

star-shaped elderberry flowers

the scent of humid pine

a bundle of purring

a forest enveloping you

alkali flats and sand hills

sandstone pinnacles

rodents hopping with nut deliveries

fresh, clear water in a stream

temperate coniferous forests

the endless prairie

the perfume of the salt air

Hawaiian sweet corn and white orchids

the precision of a Japanese garden

a dispute between arboreal rodents

the crackling sound of firewood

an uprise of weeds

green chili fields

Greenland ice cores

a lulling downpour

cones heavy in the pines

a beach rose or sprig of sea hollyhock

sunlight flushing into birds' feathers

a frog disguised as a leaf

a snowy walk in the woods

the long river-stripes of Earth

a planet appearing, clear and white

the plantar pad of a cat's foot

aardvark, a champion tunneler

a spruce cone sitting on the snow

the silver purl of a tiny stream

a hen sitting on a hay nest of eggs

wispy grass rippling

the thrilling distant howl of coyotes

erosion channels filled with snow

a full harvest moon, touchably close

Maine rocks and the churning sea

pink river dolphins

a bowerbird's nest

clouds wiping up spilled sunlight

moss clinging to rock

the snood on a turkey

a buck with beautiful antlers

clusters of violets

the sound of pinecones falling

a patchwork of cirrus clouds

the air before a thunderstorm

being knee-deep in wildflowers

the glossy fronds of palm trees

the scent of Provence lavender

soft winter sunlight

a gigantic Spring moon

the peak of a mountain

the sun setting over the water

houseplants that remind you of spring

geese raising their young in a park

a starling murmuration at sunset

a dolphinet, a female dolphin

the rocky steps of a waterfall

the sound of a bee in flight

rock polish, striations, and grooves

the birth of an island

snowfall in the afternoon

Japanese barberry in winter

guided nature hikes

birds contributing nesting material

redbuds and dogwoods in bloom

the trembling of a leaf

an emerald lake of quiet serenity

European bee-eater birds

a consortium of crabs

the mild warmth of spring

dark slimy mats of leaves

cobbles, pebbles, and flagstones

the first flight of birds after rain

the croaking of the resident frog

bees crawling across flower petals

the bright red corn poppy

when the crickets start to hum

bees waking in the hive

the twilight serenade of farm dogs

a nest of birds in a horse's stall

the Alaskan rain forest

the color of ripe strawberries

clear pebbles of rain

the nightingale's song

the nocturnal bird of prey, the owl

lilies by lantern light

the air sharp with nature smells

the warm reddish-purple of the clover

a rain-dappled pond

the superfluity of nature

deer tracks in fresh-fallen snow

the smell of a lemon orchard

snow dust and sparkle

graceful cypress trees

geese crossing the road

a bullfrog in the cattails

bare feet in the ocean

soft, cuddly pandas

gigantic crystals in a cavern or mine

a pack of porcupines

autumn arriving while you sleep

bird footprints in the snow

the minstrelsy of gnats and mosquitoes

sea or mountain air

ruffles of whitecaps

blue haze caused by terpenes

mixed sun and shade flowers

the natural colors of Alpaca wool

tilted strata

a pasture of horses

perfect little raspberries

the soft muted colors of seashells

leaves shedding before they turn

the tumbling well of space

when you can sense it snowing

blackbirds in the marsh

wild grasses growing in tufts

crisp November oak leaves

nighttime rainbows (moonbows)

goats in argan trees

a rumble of thunder

farmland overlooking a tidal pond

the chatter of swallows

fields of mustard yellow

farmland—nature's highways

dark pillars of sylvan aisles

a clifftop above a pounding sea

deer standing frozen, waiting

weather residing in the troposphere

rearrangement of the clouds

a raft of hooded mergansers

the sun rearing its radiant head

western wheat grass

the lip of a volcano

bright pink sunsets

the gentle spiral of a conch shell

woodpecker Morse code

crystalline tree branches

sky-high mountain passes

flat, dark water under a pale blue sky

ash trees losing their winged keys

silvery green moss

the sound of corn growing

a wasp being thwarted by a window

the colors of ponderosa bark at sunset

swans flying along the sun's path

a long nature walk

nebulae and star clusters

birds of prey sweeping

a flock of pigeons homing

little bulbs busily flowering

the patterns of the forest

the subtleties and nuances of rocks

burnished autumn roses

red berries next to green holly leaves

when fog begins to go up into the air

every amazing sunrise

the fresh water of an iceberg

stars, the streetlights of eternity

the moon, Earth's night light

snow dusting the cobblestones

tadpoles skittering into reeds

groves of lemon trees

moisture for moss and lichen

the sleeping patterns of fish

a field of bluebonnets

patches of scrub forest

mad pushes of waves upon the land

camels down on folded legs

when it sounds like spring

butterflies in October

evolution by natural selection

when the mist is on the lake

the call of the raven

polar bears being mainly left-pawed

a seabound boulder

the Precambrian to Devonian periods

a walk down a pine-needled path

coyotes saluting the moon

the buzzing of bees

the sleeping habits of birds

a twirled vine looping its way skyward

the indomitable forsythia

hopeful plots of bare dirt

clouds gliding past the moon

pussy willow catkins

the sky during a lightning storm

dew on leaves, crystal, opalescent

smooth glacier-polished outcroppings

multicolored mosses and lichens

the shape and pattern of the fields

a river yielding salmon and trout

flowers' last flush

the blue full moon

a whole tree alive with birds

the spider's skill at weaving

cold air plus warm sun

daffodils waking a grassy woodland

a gentle, rippling stream

pockets of light rain

icy mountain nights

the colors of falling leaves

oranges full of juice

the winter entrance to the beehive

ladybugs hibernating in groups

early morning frost on trees

a fox in the goldenrod

walks in cool glens of ferns

the cliffs of Big Sur

tide pools at high tide

baby pelicans and flying pelicans

the unreachable top of a tree

the happy pattern of a butterfly

nature's dens and crevasses

rain in the mountains

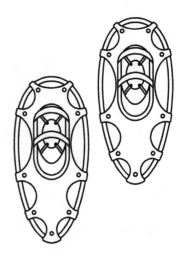

a crystalline night sky

the sleeping position of horses

heavy blackberry blooms

the salt-and-pepper look of granite

the nuthatch cracking his breakfast

herons flying over rice fields

tie-dyed blue-green sea

a big moon playing peekaboo

the sound produced by a camel

an orange rising sun

antique golden roses

the sweet spicy odor of shaggy juniper

abscission of trees in the fall

a jungle walk at night

green buds fat but unburst

a dusting of white on the evergreens

low yellow autumn or winter sunlight

two chipmunks in a chase

an unusual bird at the feeder

soil rich as chocolate

the river finding its way to the ocean

the sound of a sudden gust of wind

pigeons seeing in slow motion

the tiny red eyeshine of spiders

sage wafting from a hidden garden

bees on a sunny autumn day

how small life is for other animals

the cells of a honeycomb

the scrim of the clouds

a campfire under the stars

the stern curve of a mountain slope

a whale's tail in the ocean waves

the sea taking on a gray marbled look

massive Holsteins grazing close

the stark beauty of the boreal forest

birds going about their birdy lives

the morning sun lighting up a mountain

cackles in a hen house

green peninsulas and natural springs

fish zigzagging through the water

stars in the night sky

the end of a storm

goats dawdling in the road

oceans with crashing waves

pine boughs sagging with snow

the perfect design of an egg

static soaring by birds

a variegated garden

roadside berry bushes

blackbirds on a winter lawn

air silken and golden with light

a giant ice disk churning in a river

the brightness of the summer sun

geological phenomena

a picnic on soft grass

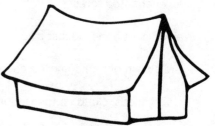

the velvety skin of a peach

a gull circling in the wind

a wild boar foraging

the breeze hitting a bit of bough

atmospheric haze clearing

hills of crumpled velvet

leaves moving in the hot breeze

nature teaching us about change

a panther walking to-and-fro on a limb

ferns growing in the shade

a mass of Monarch butterflies

a walk in the cool moonlight

long-threaded moss

the folds and wrinkles of leaves

a sun-dappled lagoon

what the animal world has to teach us

coconut palms that speckle the shores

the delicate hooves of a goat

an enchanted forest

an ancient honey locust tree

the splash of rain against a cheek

cloud seeds, cloud condensation nuclei

a whale yawn

the mockingbird's tones

a cat's four rows of whiskers

a French parterre garden

houseplants that bloom in the winter

a downy woodpecker at the suet

a duck-billed platypus

heirloom tomatoes grown from seeds

a gathering of chipmunks

crickets playing dead

a little crab scurrying

the screes of a mountain

a fluffy mound of clouds

nature in a white sleep

a piece of nature's artwork

cornflowers' simplicity

salmon running in a mountain stream

a frozen pond sparkling with rime

the tawny flush of Midwestern wheat

a small island in a river or lake

leaves snuggled around bushes

when it rains, looking for rainbows

a thin spring rain

the roots of plants

the random elegance of clouds

deer traversing the garden

how nature always appears new to us

thick granite walls

the three-toed sloth

pear, nut, and peach trees

the dwarf mongoose

gulls gossiping and chattering

grass popping up after a rain

white stones in a brook

a field mouse tunneling out of sight

grassy tufts, a great expanse of field

lavender, blue in the breeze

small treasures found in nature

a tender wildflower deep in the wood

comets seen frequently, like Encke's

nature's mighty law

knap, the crest or summit of a hill

sponges swaying on a reef

the headlong enthusiasm of a horse

prairie dogs' towns

the fluffy dandelion plume

the color of a marmalade cat

wind wagging the weeds

the shell-like curves of deer hooves

stars paling in the morning sky

the clear, deep lakes of Maine

living on a planet in the Goldilocks Zone

flocks of flamingos

a frog sitting on a lily pad

the badger in the backyard

sky a softening blue

the taut ears of deer

a shadow caused by a cloud

the willow-draped banks of a river

the first tiny green leaves of spring

brightly colored hummingbirds

snow making everything look clean

salt air breezing across your cheeks

snow on oyster beds at low tide

a chipmunk zipping by

the height of pumpkin season

a slow breeze on an autumn day

the biodiversity of sunlit reefs

a plant that is one of a kind

an enthusiastic cat bath

the twitch of furred skin

abalone clinging to rocks

tree peepers' song as you drive by

a flowering crabapple tree

the patter of unspoilt nature

an aerial view of maturing rice fields

dewclaws on dogs and cats

winterberries and bittersweet

celandine sprouting wild in the garden

ducks gathering their ducklings

birds singing joyfully in the rain

patches of spired blue flowers

the muffled quiet of snowfall

howler monkeys at dawn

sunny days replacing gray

the rough and sturdy oyster shell

the crater of a glaciated volcano

Old Man Winter

deer walking upon the mountains

stumps of an interglacial forest

the buttercup family

aestivation of animals

Australian cattle dogs or heelers

skies of changing light

pure drifts of silken powder snow

a clamshell half opened

wet earth warming in the sun

tumbleweeds huddled together

snowflakes absorbing sound waves

rushes and cattails in marshland

pure white dalmatians at birth

the horizon

ranger-led canoe trips

monocotyledons and dicotyledons

lilacs blooming in the dooryard

stars in the winter sky

lime blossoms

that feeling of autumn in the air

the smell of wild strawberries

ancient plane trees

the full Worm Moon

the hushed murmur of surf

beautiful ice bubbles frozen in a lake

breakers on the beach

the wind knocking an apple from a tree

bees in the flowers in quest of nectar

brown pelicans skimming water

a mole scurrying over the snow

the mist of ocean spray

the pattern of shadows on the rocks

gray sky turning fully blue

the metronome of rain

the husky chirping of house sparrows

jack-in-the-pulpit

frozen lakes beginning to sing

birds diving for fallen food

woods gaping like an open mouth

smooth blue muscles of wave

leaves retained through the winter

ripples in a river

leaves and acorns crunching underfoot

natural sea sponges

the fragrance of winter flowers

icebergs, Ice Age cathedrals

the slow chiseling of water on rock

El Niño-less years

a ripe pear, tender near the stem

crimson blueberry fields

deep red pomegranate

bleached high noon in New Mexico

colorful autumn vegetables

a butterfly in the winter woods

the cry of a predator bird

bioluminescent plankton

serene sunlit forests

seafloor spreading

the warmth of a daylily

worm compost

a pyramid dune with rippled flanks

how the sun washes the earth

grapes growing in an arbor

a soft, moist flower petal

magnificent tulip trees

nature's raw power

beach sand holding in a summer storm

sea lapping at your toes

tall mountain gum trees

where the condor soars

a wilderness of sand dunes

the geometry of river systems

woods coming alive

the honey-seeking bee

the almost-no-bugs season

a sea of yellow buttercups

spiderwebs drifting off beams

the aubergine drapery of the forest

a deep periwinkle sky

the damp coldness of misty regions

lava beds holding fossil treasures

a small plant or tree, growing

big flowers, little bugs

a romantic rose garden

the shades of nightfall

a mother skunk marching her kits

an aerial view of a forest

just staring up into the sky

moss-covered tree roots

the tawny frogmouth bird

delicate wood sorrel in a bed of moss

a vein of gold ore

the leaf shapes of specific trees

the pervading scent of grain

birds singing after a storm

an expedition to Antarctica

water in the desert

bird cries echoing in the autumn air

late light slanting in the afternoon

the earth echoing the sky

heart-stoppingly beautiful trees

delicate pink hydrangea

the cool wind of spring

clouds rearranging themselves

the skeleton of a desiccated leaf

cosmic background radiation

the slow coming of evening

an autumn-brown beach

hieroglyphic tracks on snow

a lake shimmering in the distance

a dip in a waterfall pool

raptors haunting rocky heights

a sunflower taller than you

how the noonday sun flattens

the streamlet's flow

cloudscape reflections on water

woods moist in early spring

mushrooms growing under trees

ocean waves in their rhythm

daisies and lotuses blooming at dawn

fractures in the crust of a lava lake

the blue helmet of the sky

pinnate compound leaves

the quirky decisions of small animals

leaves dancing in the breeze

sunrise on a volcano

the branch and bark of trees

boulder fields overlooking trails

April's full pink moon

an almond branch against the sky

a horse's signature gait

glimpses of nature in the city

a plant that is 1,000 years old

the smell of wet violets in spring

warm sun and gentle rain

gorgeous autumn afternoons

nematodes and rotifers

a dandelion fluff explosion

ponds and blueberry thickets

flowers waking up, getting out of bed

marshlands aglow with twilight sun

a feather left on the shore

the sounds of winter

seahorse mating rituals

a flock of white aspen trees

the lingonberry or mountain cranberry

what the air smells like in the Arctic

a large-flowered cactus

wild orange lilies

butterflies emerging from hibernation

dramatic mountain peaks

a two-spotted ladybug

prickly parched grass

a sundog or fire rainbow

fledglings in the nest

a garden in its flush of green glory

the weird sounds that birds make

mist from a mountain cave

the sinter crust of a hot spring

natural rock chimneys

flowers blooming overnight

the first flower bulbs popping

light making color visible

river eroding rock—slowly

a light snow at bedtime

rainbows thrown up by waterfalls

an English cottage garden

a bird putting on a show

ripe grass in need of a comb and brush

the surface of a leaf, the pagina

a network of fractures in ice

the reptilian prowess of an alligator

an aerial view of a waterfall

butterflies tasting with their feet

horses' sheer energy

boisterous, exuberant Canadian geese

a cold breeze off the sea

the active volcanoes of Alaska

the yellow-flowered cotton plant

a continental margin

the vibrant trunk of a tree

the winter solstice

animals scratching their ears

a huge seagrass forest

bare trees creaking

majestic wedge-tailed eagles circling

a badger retreating to the set

moisture piercing a seed's skin

icicles on a waterfall

clouds forming into friendly shapes

Alaska's more than 3 million lakes

the escape play of horses

Canada geese in a V

errant wild turkey

the dark color of merlot grapes

the energetic rushing of a stream

leaves gliding and swooping

thousands of hectares of waving grass

ambrosial fog stretched over a river

a planet's size to the naked eye

fresh new tulips emerging

blossoms grounded by pelting rain

Mexican star bulbs

a warren of rabbits

red geraniums in the wild

sandstone of ancient stream beds

a lone cypress tree

alders spreading, unchecked

that special star you wish on

in-like-a-lion weather

what we learn from fossils

the shy snuffling of a hedgehog

miles of dark trees

the branch tips of blue spruce

the mystery and peace of the forest

two-note birdcalls

the different textures of a river

saffron crocus flowers

a spider plant sending off shoots

the explosion of mums in a fall garden

the icy tap of snow against the window

algae streaks in a saline lake

a fat squirrel chewing on a pear

cold, gray, wet, muddy mornings

fish full of fish happiness

a bird feeder where you can watch

swans gliding across a still lake

bees bumbling more slowly

the oak sleeping in the acorn

white birch trees in fall colors

Antarctic fishes and fur seals

ice worms

flowers kissing the air

roses tangling in the beech hedge

mass coral spawning

a cock crowing in its farmyard

beach lichen

a tidal beach with oyster beds

the screech of the ground squirrel

a bird released from its egg

barnacle-studded stones

shells at low tide

breeze wet with salt

crevices of cliff rock

bears hibernating in dens

a jay jabbering outside the window

the peacefulness of a winter wood

the smell of sweet fern

a submerged reef island

white garden heliotrope

coal in the process of formation

chicks chirping for food

the background sounds of nature

fresh snow on a red bridge

a cat in a puddle of sun

an ongoing geologic work of art

a particularly stalwart tree

the marsh at midnight

colors of the desert sun

overgrown grass in a damp orchard

palmate and pinnate leaves

windswept offshore islands

cool-season annual flowers

mountain reflections on the water

the searing light of sunrise

gently waving fans of red coral

a canyon waterfall

the stripes on cat legs

a slightly angry volcano

flowers perking up in the sun

the time of wild cherry blossoms

nature wearing her prettiest clothes

an anthill busy at work

wind and the loose leaves

plump, open red roses

thick geological strata

the last gray winter mornings

the crash and caterwaul of the sea

puddles full of leaves

a clear, high-pitched bird call

a retreat in the mountains

the sluggish waters of a pond

rainbows looping over the clouds

the scent of bay trees

sap, a tree's lifeblood

glossy conkers on a chestnut tree

small-clawed otters or leopard geckos

the small events of the natural world

a small brook in a green glade

the Carboniferous to Permian periods

deer depressions in the grass

millions-of-years-old shell fossils

alpenglow

the smell of dew in the morning

bull rays gliding along a sandy bottom

puffins and craggy cliffs

a shimmering cloud of fish

a magnificent rainbow

green lacewing eggs

dark rumpled chains of seaweed

the secret language of trees

thickets of oregano and sage

an elephant's trunk raised in greeting

polygons in the tundra

a rigid chandelier of blue icicles

songbirds at the feeder

the science of lakes and fresh water

a secret robin's nest found

the coo of a pigeon

bees that do not sting

leaf peeping in autumn

an animal's free forest life

the inevitability of falling leaves

nature as your teacher

pigeons in a quandary

a pumpkin field in October

gourds and Indian corn

rain forest colors

jet streams on winding courses

a single thread spun by a spider

snowflakes changing a landscape

moss winding around tree trunks

seed puffs blowing through the air

moraine bands on a glacier

a robin singing at sunset

the sea's withdrawal

a just-bloomed flower

reindeer eating bananas

two squirrels hugging in the backyard

an acorn super-year, a mast year

blowsy pink peonies dappled in dew

moonbeams and stardust

geraniums thriving on windowsills

sap from rubber trees

a back lawn with mountain views

trees overgrown with moss

Earth, rolling from west to east

a sunrise across a mountain lake

snow in the clouds

the persistence of brambles

mushrooms in an unplowed field

horses snorting at one another

WAYS NATURE MAKES US SMILE IN THE NATIONAL PARKS

Acadia National Park (Maine)
- bike carriage roads
- whale watching
- dramatic sea cliffs and secluded coves
- the Wild Gardens
- Cadillac Mountain

Arches National Park (Utah)
- small honeycomb formations called tafoni
- giant balanced rocks
- taking the Fiery Furnace Loop Tour
- a nature story beginning roughly 65 million years ago
- desert varnish where water cascades off cliffs

Badlands National Park (South Dakota)
- one of the world's richest fossil beds
- bison, bighorn sheep, prairie dogs, and black-footed ferrets
- driving the Badlands Loop Road
- hardy grasses surviving where other plants cannot
- hills of ecru and sepia

Big Bend National Park (Texas)
- a blend of mountains, desert, water, and Wild West
- the Rio Grande's huge left turn
- rafting Santa Elena Canyon
- riverside rock pools
- the desert coming alive with sagebrush and ocotillo's colors

Biscayne National Park (Florida)
- aquamarine waters, emerald islands, and fish-bejeweled coral reefs
- a Sail, Paddle, Snorkel, and Island Visit tour
- an extensive mangrove forest
- seagrass beds, sponges, manatees, and sea turtles
- a diver's paradise through transitional islands of coral and sand

Black Canyon of the Gunnison (Colorado)
- a park big enough to be overwhelming and intimate enough to feel the pulse of time
- the Gunnison River sculpting a vertical wilderness of rock, water, and sky
- Black Canyon's night skies
- descending the Gunnison Route
- spotted fawns of mule deer

Bryce Canyon National Park (Utah)
- the hoodoos (tall spires of stone)
- a hike with views of multihued sandstone cliffs
- millions of years of wind and water erosion
- hiking the Figure-8 Combination
- Rainbow Point's layers of pink, gray, white, vermilion, and chocolate

Canyonlands National Park (Utah)
- a giant jigsaw puzzle of mesas, buttes, arches, pinnacles, and deep canyons
- centuries-old petroglyphs covering rock formations
- mountain biking White Rim Road
- the red-and-white striped pinnacles of the Needles district
- preserved Anasazi ruins

Capitol Reef National Park (Utah)
- the Waterpocket Fold, a wrinkle on the earth extending 100 miles
- historic orchards blooming in spring
- exploring Cottonwood Wash, a slot canyon
- buff-pink Entrada Sandstone formation, deposited 160 million years ago
- eroded sandstone shapes that look like ornate Gothic cathedrals

Carlsbad Caverns National Park (New Mexico)
- high ancient sea ledges, flowering cactus, and deep canyons
- hidden below, 119 caves formed from dissolved limestone
- a rare wooded riparian area designated as an Important Bird Area
- the development of caves much older than the surrounding landscape
- taking the Guided King's Palace Tour

Channel Islands National Park (California)
- kayaking through sea caves
- sea caves and surf breaks and a five-island archipelago
- a water-filled grotto that is a mosaic of rocks, moss, and algae
- cobblestone beaches and olive groves
- Torrey Pines, a grove of the rarest native pine

Congaree National Park (South Carolina)
- an expanse of old-growth bottomland hardwood forest
- canoeing or kayaking Cedar Creek
- a 50-mile designated recreational paddling trail
- meanders and sandbars
- prescribed burns helping certain ecosystems thrive

Crater Lake National Park (Oregon)
- cruising the Scenic Rim Drive
- a spectacular segment of the Pacific Crest Trail
- towering pinnacles and fossil fumaroles under sheets of volcanic pumice
- gazing down into the deep blue belly of the lake
- an almost total absence of pollutants in a lake

Cuyahoga Valley National Park (Ohio)
- a park that is a poster child for waterway restoration
- canoeing Horseshoe Pond and Kendall Lake with a guide
- a park hosting geocaching adventures
- stops along the Lake Erie Birding Trail
- fly fishing the Cuyahoga River

Death Valley National Park (California, Nevada)
- hiking Mosaic Canyon

- towering peaks frosted with winter snow
- rare rainstorms bringing vast fields of wildflowers
- lush oases harboring tiny fish and being a refuge for wildlife
- the extremes and striking contrasts of a below-sea-level basin

Denali National Park and Preserve (Alaska)
- central Alaska's legendary wildlife
- biking Denali Park Road
- boreal forest, tundra, wild rivers, and glaciers
- an enormous granite pluton thrust up by plate tectonics
- six million acres of wild land bisected by one ribbon or road

Dry Tortugas National Park (Florida)
- sooty terns and brown noddies making nests and raising their young
- a park 99 percent water, with seven small islands
- picturesque blue waters, superlative coral reefs, and marine life
- swimming and snorkeling at a national park
- camping on Garden Key

Everglades National Park (Florida)
- being in one of the world's largest tropical wetlands
- taking a guided airboat tour
- padding along the shore of Florida Bay
- the weeklong journey between Flamingo and Everglades City
- viewing crocodiles, turtles, and bird life at close, but safe, range

Gates of the Arctic National Park (Alaska)
- a national park with no roads, so you have to raft and backpack
- intact ecosystems where people have lived off the land for over 10,000 years
- wild rivers meandering glacier-carved valleys
- caribou migrating in Brooks Range
- endless summer night fading into aurora-lit night skies of winter

Gateway Arch National Park (Missouri)
- a park reflecting the westward expansion of the US
- an urban national park
- taking a tram ride to the top of Gateway Arch

- a fantastic view of the mighty Mississippi River
- soaking in the environment using all five senses

Glacier National Park (Montana)
- living and fossilized stromatolites
- a high-country wonderland of rock, ice, water, and wood
- overnighting at Granite Park Chalet
- a juvenile cougar or hoary marmot looking out from the brush
- Rocky Mountain goats clinging to the cliffs

Glacier Bay National Park and Preserve (Alaska)
- Alaska's Inside Passage
- a land reborn, a world returning to life, a living lesson in resilience
- taking the day boat, a park-sanctioned cruise ship
- wilderness that is remote, dynamic, and intact
- a natural place that offers human solitude

Grand Canyon National Park (Arizona)
- scenic viewpoints at Pipe Creek Vista, Mather Point, and Yavapai Point
- rowing the milk chocolate-colored Colorado River
- a sacred place of pilgrimage and prayer
- International Dark Sky Park status
- the thought of hiking rim-to-rim

Grand Teton National Park (Wyoming)
- snowcapped peaks reflected in fjord-like lakes
- serrated granite peaks, perfectly proportioned
- Snake River and Jackson Lake
- the Antelope Flats
- backpacking the Teton Crest Trail

Great Basin National Park (Nevada)
- walking among ancient bristlecone pine
- exploring mysterious subterranean passages in the Lehman Caves
- fierce summer afternoon thunderstorms
- sagebrush, grasslands, pinyon-juniper woods, and ponderosa pine
- hiking the Bristlecone Grove and Glacier Trail

Great Sand Dunes National Park and Preserve (Colorado)

- a national park with no limitations, timed entries, or reservations required
- the tallest sand dunes in North America
- sand sledding and sandboarding
- splashing in Medano Creek
- climbing the High Dune on First Ridge

Great Smoky Mountains National Park (North Carolina, Tennessee)

- biking Cades Cove on a vehicle-free day
- the North Carolina quiet side of the Smokies
- synchronous fireflies flashing en masse
- horseback riding in the most visited national park
- the thick vegetation that emits natural mist

Guadalupe Mountains National Park (Texas)

- the world's most extensive Permian fossil reef
- summitting Guadalupe Peak
- salt flats, creosote bushes, and honey mesquite
- bigtooth maple, velvet ash, chinkapin oak
- springs recharged by mountain streams

Haleakalā National Park (Hawaii)

- hiking Keonehe'ehe'e (Sliding Sands) Trail
- an ever-changing interplay of clouds, sky, and volcanic desert
- a night sky almost devoid of air pollution and urban lights
- walking across a crater floor
- the strange *hinahina* (silver-sword) plants

Hawai'i Volcanoes National Park (Hawaii)

- glowing lava flows, wind, rain, and waves
- pockets of rain forest and grassland shelter rare in Hawaii
- red-hot lava rushing across land and into the Pacific Ocean
- Kīlauea and Mauna Loa, two of the most active volcanoes
- taking the Circle of Fire Helicopter Tour

Hot Springs National Park (Arkansas)

- ancient thermal springs nearly 4,000 years old
- safe, cold thermal spring fountains

- soaking in mineral water
- mosses and blue-green algae shaded by trees
- listening to the sounds of running natural water

Indiana Dunes National Park (Indiana)
- thousands of acres of beach, marsh, and hardwood forest
- wind and waves shaping the land and habitats
- hiking the Cowles Bog Trail
- building sandcastles and admiring lake sunsets
- a river during a summer steelhead run

Isle Royale National Park (Michigan)
- paddling and portaging interior lakes
- Mount Franklin's views across the water to Ontario
- cedar swamps, beaver ponds, and rocky cliffs
- backpacking the Greenstone Ridge Trail
- a rugged, isolated island far from communities

Joshua Tree National Park (California)
- the Mojave and Colorado Deserts, two distinct ecosystems, meeting
- rock climbing huge mounds with a guide
- short hikes in a hot area
- Joshua trees in their many different forms
- the yucca's grotesque appearance

Katmai National Park and Preserve (Alaska)
- geothermal landscape, crater lake, and sprawling lava fields
- salmon-snatching grizzly bears
- trails where you can go days or weeks without seeing another human
- gray wolves
- hundreds of prehistoric archaeological sites

Kenai Fjords National Park (Alaska)
- a look at what most of North America was like 12,000 years ago
- icebergs floating across fjords along a coastline
- kayaking the Aialik Glacier

- an Iditarod dogsledding trail
- humpbacks, orcas, puffins, sea otters, sea lions

Kings Canyon National Park (California)
- the General Grant Tree, called the nation's Christmas tree
- western juniper and foxtail pine
- the Fallen Monarch and the Centennial Stump
- backpacking the Evolution Valley Loop
- spotting a California condor

Kobuk Valley National Park (Alaska)
- caribou tracks crisscrossing sculpted dunes
- walking across the Great Kobuk Sand Dunes
- wild alliums growing along the Kobuk River (the Onion Portage)
- an ancient and current corridor for people and wildlife
- wolves and brown bears following a caribou migration

Lake Clark National Park and Preserve (Alaska)
- getting to a national park by boat or plane that lands on the lake
- sockeye red salmon returning via Newhalen River
- Crescent Lake, deep in the wild
- yearling cubs resting on a beach
- paddling and hiking around the Twin Lakes

Lassen Volcanic National Park (California)
- summitting Lassen Peak
- a place where all four volcano types occur
- snow-capped volcanoes
- roadless wilderness to explore on foot
- a view across lava beds to the Painted Dunes and Mount Lassen

Mammoth Cave National Park (Kentucky)
- exploring a cave in the longest known cave system in the world
- a bison range
- taking an Introduction to Caving course
- a UNESCO World Heritage Site and International Biosphere Reserve
- trails traversed by horse

Mesa Verde National Park (Colorado)
- a home to a thousand species; several that live nowhere else on earth
- touring Cliff Palace
- well-preserved cliff dwellings in blocks of hard sandstone
- a short walk to the highest point in a park
- astronomical observations drawing on natural features in the landscape

Mount Rainier National Park (Washington)
- stately Mount Rainier's snowcapped backdrop to Puget Sound
- grayish tree trunks glistening silver in a certain light
- trails climbing steadily upward through wildflower-filled tundra
- following a guide rope up Mount Rainier
- the most glaciated peak in the contiguous United States, spawning five major rivers

National Park of American Samoa (American Samoa)
- a park halfway between Hawaii and New Zealand
- hiking to a hidden beach
- giant waves crashing into steep volcanic cliffs
- the most distant unit of the NPS having coconut palm trees
- surreal peaks that look as if they were painted on the sky

New River Gorge National Park and Preserve (West Virginia)
- a rugged whitewater river flowing through deep canyons
- one of the oldest rivers on the continent
- whitewater rafting the Lower New River
- skinks, wild turkeys, raptors, and ravens
- a wildflower art contest

North Cascades National Park Complex (Washington)
- the numerous peaks, glaciers, and lakes spangling the park
- lesser-trampled trailed and solitary lakeshores
- 100 percent wilderness that can be accessed only on foot
- visiting Stehekin
- moss covering tree branches

Olympic National Park (Washington)
- a million primeval acres
- walking or backpacking in Hoh Rainforest
- a wild Pacific coastline that seems totally untouched by humans
- mineral pools, tide pools, harbor seals, porpoises, and sea otters
- a great spot for fish to spawn in autumn

Petrified Forest National Park (Arizona)
- the solitude and adventure of backcountry hiking
- hiking the Blue Mesa Trail, a one-mile lollipop loop
- bunchgrass, blue grama, and sacaton grasses
- highly eroded and colorful badlands
- fossils from the Late Triassic

Pinnacles National Park (California)
- where multiple volcanoes erupted, flowed, and slid
- rare talus caves and California red-legged frogs
- towering rock spires teeming with life
- hiking Condor Gulch to High Peaks Loop
- prairie and peregrine falcons, golden eagles, and the California condor

Redwood National and State Park (California)
- cathedral-like groves of the tallest trees
- tranquil lagoons and rolling grasslands
- the secret location of Hyperion Tree
- whale watching from bluff overlooks
- a reservation to hike Tall Trees Grove

Rocky Mountain National Park (Colorado)
- the multiple trips to experience a huge park
- experiencing the highest national park and the Continental Divide
- cliffs sheltering herds of bighorn sheep
- glaciers tucked into cirques and ancient bristlecone pine
- climbing Longs Peak or taking a day hike to Chasm Lake

Saguaro National Park (Arizona)
- the largest cacti, the giant saguaro, silhouetted at sunset
- Sonoran Desert landscape

- the Madrean Sky Islands
- hiking up Wasson Peak
- the Pinal Schist and 1.4-billion-year-old granites

Sequoia National Park (California)
- backpacking to Redwood Meadow Grove
- being dwarfed by trees, like General Sherman
- Moro Rock offering a bird's-eye view looking down on giant sequoias
- an underground wonderland of stalagmites and stalactites
- the world's largest trees and 300 native animal species

Shenandoah National Park (Virginia)
- driving Skyline Drive
- wood hollows, breezy summits, waterfalls, and mountain streams
- Dark Hollows Falls
- standing above the clouds, white wisps surrounding the hills
- wooded highlands offering refuge from heat and humidity

Theodore Roosevelt National Park (North Dakota)
- a place that sparks passion for exploring and conserving wild places
- wooded gullies along the Little Missouri River
- prairie flora and fauna
- exploring the west bank's wilderness area and petrified forest
- spotting the park's herd of longhorn cattle

Virgin Islands National Park (U.S. Virgin Islands)
- pristine coastline and countryside
- wild iguana basking in the sun
- scuba diving to see fish and corals
- a forest spangled with mango, kapok, and other large tropical trees
- sea turtles in grassy underwater meadows

Voyageurs National Park (Minnesota)
- captaining a houseboat
- the Northern Lights when the sky is clear
- a place of transition between land and aquatic ecosystems

- canoeing the Boundary Waters Area Wilderness
- snowshoe hiking in a park

White Sands National Park (New Mexico)
- great wavelike dunes of glistening gypsum
- an inspirational moment in an untamable land
- hiking the Alkali Flat Trail
- primitive backcountry camping sites
- the silence and solitude of a huge dunefield

Wind Cave National Park (South Dakota)
- taking a Wild Cave Tour
- roaming bison and elk
- Wind Cave, one of the longest and most complex in the world
- following a herd of animals
- a place very significant in wildlife conservation

Wrangell-St. Elias National Park and Preserve (Alaska)
- America's largest national park
- lynx and loon, cranberry and rose, black bear and red fox
- ice climbing the Root Glacier
- moonlit willow thickets laced with hare trails
- a grove of paper birch glowing yellow on the hillside

Yellowstone National Park (Wyoming, Montana, Idaho)
- thermal pools, sinter terraces, and a grand canyon
- geyser gazing
- preserving, rather than paving, Mother Nature's treasures
- the wildlife, the massive canyon, the simmering volcanic underbelly
- a blend of land and water, forest and field, wildlife and geothermal features

Yosemite National Park (California)
- viewing the valley for the first time, all the way to Half Dome (or hiking it)
- using binoculars to see El Capitan
- the sheer height from which Yosemite Falls descends
- Ahwahnee Meadow on the valley floor
- Mirror Lake reflecting monoliths and sunset by the Tuolumne River

Zion National Park (Utah)
- the precipitous hike up Angels Landing
- canyon frogs and tiny Zion snails
- the Great White Throne rock face
- riding horses through vermillion cliffs
- the Temple of Sinawava, a colossal natural amphitheater

APPENDIX
National Park List

Acadia National Park
American Samoa National Park
Arches National Park
Badlands National Park
Big Bend National Park
Biscayne National Park
Black Canyon of the Gunnison National Park
Bryce Canyon National Park
Canyonlands National Park
Capitol Reef National Park
Carlsbad Caverns National Park
Channel Islands National Park
Congaree National Park
Crater Lake National Park
Cuyahoga Valley National Park
Death Valley National Park
Denali National Park and Preserve
Dry Tortugas National Park
Everglades National Park
Gates of the Arctic National Park and Preserve
Glacier National Park
Glacier Bay National Park and Preserve
Grand Canyon National Park
Grand Teton National Park
Great Basin National Park
Great Sand Dunes National Park and Preserve
Great Smoky Mountains National Park
Guadalupe Mountains National Park

Haleakalā National Park
Hawaii Volcanoes National Park
Hot Springs National Park
Indiana Dunes National Park
Isle Royale National Park
Joshua Tree National Park
Katmai National Park and Preserve
Kenai Fjords National Park
Kings Canyon National Park
Kobuk Valley National Park
Lake Clark National Park and Preserve
Lassen Volcanic National Park
Mammoth Cave National Park
Mesa Verde National Park
Mount Rainier National Park
New River Gorge National Park and Preserve
North Cascades National Park
Olympic National Park
Petrified Forest National Park
Pinnacles National Park
Redwood National and State Parks
Rocky Mountain National Park
Saguaro National Park
Sequoia National Park
Shenandoah National Park
Theodore Roosevelt National Park
Virgin Islands National Park
Voyageurs National Park
White Sands National Park
Wind Cave National Park
Wrangell-St. Elias National Park and Preserve
Yellowstone National Park
Yosemite National Park
Zion National Park

ABOUT THE AUTHOR

Dr. Barbara Ann Kipfer is a lexicographer, author, archaeologist, hiker, and former sports writer. She is the author of more than seventy books, including *Hiking Is Fundamental*, *Hiking Ruins of Southern New England* (with Nick Bellantoni), *Outdoor Life Lists*, *Archaeologist's Fieldwork Guide* 2nd Edition, *Encyclopedic Dictionary of Archaeology* 2nd Edition, *14,000 Things to Be Happy About*, and *1,001 Ways to Live Wild*.

Dr. Kipfer holds a PhD in archaeology (Greenwich University), a BS in physical education (Valparaiso University), a PhD and MPhil in linguistics (University of Exeter), and an MA and PhD in Buddhist studies (Akamai University). She is a Registered Professional Archaeologist. Find more of Barbara's work online at https://www.thingstobehappyabout.com.

FALCONGUIDES®

MAKE ADVENTURE YOUR STORY™

Since 1979, FalconGuides has been a trailblazer in defining outdoor exploration. Elevate your journey with contributions by top outdoor experts and enthusiasts as you immerse yourself in a world where adventure knows no bounds.

Our expansive collection spans the world of outdoor pursuits, from hiking and foraging guides to books on environmental preservation and rockhounding. Unleash your potential as we outfit your mind with unparalleled insights on destinations, routes, and the wonders that await your arrival.

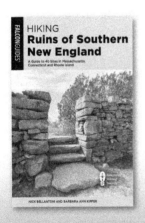

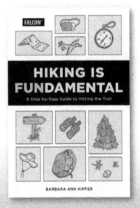

LET FALCON BE YOUR GUIDE

www.ingramcontent.com/pod-product-compliance
Lightning Source LLC
Chambersburg PA
CBHW070558030225
21169CB00004B/4